Authentic Love

(Requires Circumcision of the Heart)

Written by: Maureen & Bill Williamson

Our grateful thanks to Anita Keppinger and Nicolas Cervantes for their skillful and talented assistance in providing the cover and chapter illustrations used throughout this book.

Illustrations for cover and chapters
1,2,3, 4, 5, 7, 8, 9, 10, 12, 14, & 18
created and drawn by:
Anita Keppinger
Albany, Oregon 97321

Illustrations for chapters
6, 11, 13, 15, 16, & 17
created and drawn by:
Nicolas Cervantes
601 N. Orange Ave
Arcadia, Florida 34266
(863) 491-0749

Book layout and production by
George Payne at Write Hand Publishing
www.writehand.com

Table of Contents

PART I

~ THE LOVE ADVENTURE GOES ON ~

Chapter 1

Sholmie And The Five Hebrew Girls

Written by: Maureen Williamson

Once again I was back in Israel; this time from an extended speaking tour in America. Through a series of amazing circumstances, I had found a delightful apartment in the Jerusalem suburb of East Talpiot. Having completed the tedious job of collecting all my possessions, which I had instructed to be used in my absence,

I now stood with anticipation in front of what was to be my home.

As I fumbled in my purse for the key, surrounded by an untidy mass of personal effects, a handsome Jewish boy of about ten approached me, introduced himself as Shlomie, my new neighbor, and offered his help.

"Pleased to meet you," I said to Shlomie in my best Hebrew. Shlomie kindly proceeded to correct my grammar.

"Are you moving in here?" He asked with an astonished look on his face.

"Sure," I replied. "And you and I are going to have a lot of fun together."

He smiled a knowing smile, and said, "yes, I think so."

Sometime later, after we were better acquainted, he told me just how funny he had thought I was the first day he met me, I was a girl wearing trousers ... the first 'no-no.' And, I had paint on my face... another definite 'no-no.' I was almost too friendly for a stranger, and that did not compute well with his Jewish mind. Lastly, I was a 'Goy,' (Not a Jew). That was a mystery to him, as he had seen 'Goyim,' but never spoken to one before.

Shlomie and I got along just fine. I heard him telling a friend of his that he liked me, but that I was a terrible Hebrew student. It wasn't long before we were inseparable. We really did have a lot of fun together. He'd call his pals, and all of us would go off on hikes in the surrounding countryside. The group took to me very well, but they were informed by Shlomie that I was his girlfriend! I felt like the Pied Piper of Hamelin with all the kids around me, but still I valued every one.

From the very beginning I told them as simply as I knew how, about Jesus; all that He is, and all that He means to me. The kids were fascinated by the Bible stories, both from the New and the Old Testaments, that I was able to share with them. They knew a lot about the Old Testament, but of course, nothing about the New.

As we walked, we devised numerous projects to find unusual things on the ground. We would scrutinize them together and wonder at the marvel of creation. God was always foremost in our conversations, and I was delighted with this enthusiastic band of young souls with whom I was sharing the Word of God. The parents of these children were interested in me too. I knew the children, being children, were relating everything they heard to their parents. How incredible that a 'Goy' should be so well received!

My home was their home; and every day they would come bouncing into it. I knew, of course, that the time would come when my relationship with them, and Shlomie in particular, would be tested.

That day soon arrived. He and I were alone; he was working on some project, and I was busy with something or other. My tape recorder was on, and we were listening to some beautiful worship music. Everything was just fine, until Shlomie suddenly stood up and walked purposefully over to the tape recorder. He had his finger poised above it, and said, "I'm going to put this Jesus music off for a bit. It's always Jesus here. All your music, all you say, and all your friends. Don't you know that I am Jewish, and we don't talk about Jesus?"

I sensed that the "show-down" was coming, and I responded immediately. Taking Shlomie's trembling hand, I said, "No Shlomie, you may not turn Jesus off. Not for one moment. This is His home, and everything in it, including myself, belongs to Him. He provides everything that I have need of, including the paying of the rent, and the food we eat. He has sent me to live amongst you, and I would seriously rather die than put Him off."

Shlomie's beautiful eyes were swimming with tears. He

9

pulled away from me, stamped his foot in a defiant attitude, and said, "Well I've had enough! I'm going to tell my father and mother everything."

"I thought you had told them everything anyway, Shlomie." I replied. "But please tell them again, as I am neither ashamed of your God, nor of mine." Shlomie, sobbing, slammed the door and was gone.

An hour later there was a loud knock at my door, and I opened it to find Shlomie's mother standing there. She was unperturbed, and had only come to borrow a cup of sugar. Suddenly Shlomie appeared from behind her, dry-eyed and quite himself. He winked and said, "I could have, but I didn't. Let's go for a walk Maureen."

As young as he was, my precious friend Shlomie had come to the place where he had to make a few of his own decisions. In that hour he had obviously made them. We never had this discussion again, and he showed no further objections to the subject of Jesus, and the fact that He does continue to have pre-eminence over everything.

Jesus comes into many lives sooner or later, and just by His coming we are challenged to stand for, or against Him. How blessed are those who choose Jesus early in life, and in doing so save themselves much pain and heartache. Sadly, the more a person grows away from Christ, the more selfish he becomes. Instead of being conformed more and more into Jesus' image, as is the case with a born-again Christian, the unsaved person continues to conform to the image society expects of him.

Of the many children Shlomie brought into my home, there were five lovely Hebrew girls who were always together . I never actually saw them separated. They soaked up the atmosphere of acceptance in my home, and returned time and time again, never saying much, but always listening; of that I was very aware.

I knew all along that I was under the close scrutiny of all of them, and I felt very privileged that I was so well received by them. There was some genuine love between us. Since I was not in any way like them, there was no reason at all why the children should have been so attracted to me. Indeed what I was saying was so contrary to everything they had ever learned, and yet there I was, set amongst them, and flourishing.

My front door was closed, but locked only at night. The kids could knock and come straight in. Had this not been the case, I would have been up and down all day long. This particular afternoon however, there was a knock but nobody entered. I opened the door to see five Hebrew girls standing in a row, with very serious faces, making no effort to come inside.

"You always come straight in," I said. "So why today, are you standing out there?"

The eldest of the five spoke in reply, "We have something very important to discuss with you, and we want to do it here."

I knew instinctively that they were having the same experience that Shlomie had endured.

"So let's go in and talk," I said, indicating that they should enter.

"No," they answered. "We will stand right here. We each have a question which we want you to answer."

"Okay," I replied. "I'm ready to answer any questions that you may have."

The oldest girl nodded to the youngest as her cue to start. With the broken English of the eldest, interspersed with Hebrew, we got by.

"Why have you come here to live amongst us?" Was the first question.

My answer was: "I was sent here by Jesus Christ, for no other reason but to tell you that He is alive. Even though He died as the Jewish Sacrificial Lamb, to carry the sins of all mankind, by placing them upon Himself, so that you and I can be free to live, to serve Him, and to have a personal relationship with Him, all the days of our lives. That after you die, you will be able to go and live with Him forever. That is how much He loves you and me. That is the message that I carry to you, and that is the reason why I have come here." She nodded her head in understanding, and then nodded to the next girl.

"Why is it that we have never heard the things you talk about before?" Was the second question.

"The reason is this," I answered. "As Jews, you only ever read the Old Testament. Jesus is prophesied about many times in the Old Testament, while He is revealed completely in, the New Testament, fulfilling these prophecies. Jews, as a rule, have been taught to despise Jesus, and therefore they cannot know Him. He only reveals Himself to those who are diligent seekers.

Besides, aren't I the first Christian who has ever spoken to you?" She nodded, and gestured for the next question, number three.

"Why should we believe in Jesus?" I stopped the quiz just long enough to comment on how excellent their questions were. They were direct and bold, and in their asking, demanded the same response. How I love the Israelis, young and old. They don't "beat about the bush!" I imagined how these girls must have met together, and how wonderfully challenged they all must have been, to have formulated questions such as these. Let us never underestimate the heart and mind of a child. As a rule, they are able to perceive truth more accurately and readily than most adults. These girls were very serious, and bless their hearts, their faces showed it.

"Why should we believe in Jesus?" They challenged me.

12

"To believe in Jesus is the smartest thing that any human being can do. In fact, by believing in Jesus you can become the person God means you to be. God the Father, whom you know from the Old Covenant, said Himself at the time that John the Baptist was baptizing people in the Jordan River, *'This is my beloved Son, in whom I am well pleased; hear ye him.'* (Matthew 17:5). Believing in Jesus takes you out of the realm of the natural, into the realm of the supernatural - and I don't have to tell you, that is far more exciting."

There was no response from the girls, except another nod, and a nudge leading into question number four.... "Did the Jews kill Jesus?" This question was asked with great emotion, as I stood there praying sincerely for the wisdom I needed to answer It.

By this stage, my own eyes were swimming with tears, and trying to focus. I noticed that their's were too.

"Mankind killed Jesus, and yet, at the same time, nobody killed Jesus. He came to earth and suffered for the very purpose of dying for the sins of its people. He knew from the beginning of time that this was what He would come to do. His love is so great that He chose to lay down His life, so that every person, no matter what color or creed, whether Jew or Gentile, would, by believing in Him, inherit eternal life.

There was only one more question to go. It turned out to be the dearest and deepest theological question. It would take the study of the Bible to fully explain, and even then, it would still be a mystery. The question being, "Is Jesus God?" This is the question upon which everything hinges, and I found it interesting that it was not asked first, but last. This is the BIG question of Life, and somehow, in knowing the answer to it everything else is unimportant. How could I explain to these inquisitive minds the wonder of the Trinity, when I could hardly explain it to myself? Actually it is above explaining.

"Jesus has been around since the beginning of time. He did not just show up as a Jewish baby two thousand years ago in Bethlehem. The Father, the Son and the Holy Spirit are one, and yet three different personalities. So the answer to your question is, yes, He is God." I had intended to try and verify that statement, but the "Yes" to the question ended the debate.

For a brief moment we just stared at each other, tears running down the faces of the girls, as well as my own. The girl who had asked that final question spoke up and said, "because of this, we will not be seeing you again." They left me open-mouthed, standing in the doorway, as they walked away.

They never did come back. Sometimes I would see them on the street, and for a split second they would forget and start running towards me. Then they would stop, and turn away.

How true it is, Jesus said in John 14:6, *"I am the way, the truth, and the life: no man cometh unto the Father, but by me."* If you are not for Him, then you are against Him.

I do not believe that is the end of the story for these five Hebrew girls. Valuable seed was sown, and Scripture promises us that His Word will not return void. Seldom do we actually see the results of our effectiveness, especially in my case, where I move around so much. Still, I know that God is faithful. He is able to do exceedingly abundantly above all we ask or think, according to that power which works within us. As Christians, we are called to speak the Word, but it is the Lord, by His Holy Spirit, who will bring conviction, and it is the Lord's command to preach the Gospel to the Jew first.

I am gullible enough to believe that Shlomie may be part of that glorious group of 144,000 that the Bible speaks about. And for this I am prepared to lay down my life for the precious Jewish soul. I can also believe that the five Hebrew girls, (and also all the other dear Jewish people I have spoken to), will be part of the Bride of the Messiah, who even at this moment is being prepared for Him.

In view of the explanation of Romans 11:17-26, I am also deeply grateful to the wonderful inheritance that is mine through the Messiah, and my mission field definitely extends well into the Jewish community, as this story has reflected.

Does your heart beat for this nation too? It should, because God's Word says, 'to the Jew first, and then to the utmost parts of the earth'.

Chapter 2

Being Made New

Written by: Maureen Williamson

"This little girl is very ill, and judging from her history of bronchial difficulties since birth, I feel I must advise you that she is weak and worn down from fighting for her young life. I have seen other cases like this," said the doctor, "and I must tell you that her chances of living a normal life, and actually surviving beyond the age of seven are slim. If she can reach that age, there's a slender chance that she might outgrow this chest problem." He continued, "but that's in God's hands. The question is, will she live that long?"

This discussion between my parents and the doctor took place at my bedside. The child he referred to was me. Although weak, I felt this rush of strength welling up inside myself, as I silently cried out, "Please God, help. I want to live!"

It was hard on me as a child, and even harder on my parents, having to watch their precious daughter suffer. I had been sickly since my birth; so much so that the arches of my feet had fallen from sheer weakness, and now to top it all, I had to wear callipers. Most of the time I had my own private nurse at my side who never let me out of her sight, which added to my aggravation. My parents recall an incident when, having had so many injections and never complaining, one night I actually shouted out from the pain of the needle, "Leave me alone!" I was desperately tired of being called "Maureen, the sick child."

A few weeks before my seventh birthday I sank to my lowest ebb. I had never been so ill, and everyone was wondering if this was, indeed, the end. On the morning of my birthday it was with great joy that I rose from my sickbed, healed, transformed, made new. Although the situation was "touch and go," surely I was "touched and sent."

It is interesting to note that the number "seven" has special significance in the Bible. It is considered the Lord's number, and the King James version of the Bible states that in 300 verses, the number seven is quoted 463 times. How could the significance of that number escape anyone's notice on my seventh birthday?

A new chapter had begun in my life. I grew tall and strong, and my motto was, "Watch out world, Maureen is very much alive and well, and making up for all those wasted years!" The Sick Maureen was now, The Adventurous Maureen, whose energy and fascination for life knew no bounds. My parents were as overjoyed as I was. After hanging onto life by a thread, there followed 26 years where I thought I had life by the tail, as Sinatra would say, "doing it my way."

My childhood was spent in Rhodesia, (now known as Zimbabwe). You could say I had a privileged upbringing. We had servants and lived in affluence. I was a fashion model from the tender age of seven. At thirty-three years of age my aim was to be like Elizabeth Taylor, not only to look like her, but the part of having eight husbands really appealed to me.

A child of God somehow found her way into my most worldly jet set friends. Her name was Estelle and she shone with the light and love of God.

Estelle had experienced many difficult things in life and so had her family. Still Estelle was an over comer, and every other word seemed to be 'Jesus.' She was quick to tell me that my life was on a collision course and that I needed Jesus. I was shocked at this statement because I believed I had need of nothing and nobody. I was intrigued by her clean and uncompromising life, she was unlike any of my other friends.

Estelle kept presenting Jesus to me and I kept refusing Him, but inwardly I was hoping she would keep pressing me as I saw in her a reason for living that none of my friends knew anything about.

One day Estelle asked me once again to come to church with her. This time she said the church had grown too big for their building and was moving temporarily into a theater. Now she had my interest! A theater I related to very well. "Can I wear something wild?" I enquired.

"Sure," Estella said, "nobody is going to notice what you wear." That was a whole new concept to me. Everything I was about had to do with what I wore. My modeling career and everything that pertained to my life was based around my wardrobe. I agreed to go with Estelle to church in the theater, but I had no idea how much that single decision would be the turning point of my life.

The preacher spoke of things my ears had never heard and I found myself inching closer to the edge of my seat in fascination. Then the preacher said an amazing thing, "If there is anybody here that has not met Jesus Christ personally and would like to, please come up now."

I shot out of my chair and climbed over a few people in my urgency to get to the preacher. The place was crowded but as a matter of urgency I was nearly running, and as I did my chest felt like it was being cut open. With tears streaming down my cheeks, I felt a hand reach into my chest and remove my heart of stone and immediately replace it with a heart of flesh. *"A new heart also will I give you, and a new spirit will I put within you: and I will take away the stony heart out of your flesh, and I will give you an heart of flesh."* Ezek 36:26.

About twenty of us gathered at the altar and we listened intently as the preacher explained that it was necessary to admit we were sinners in need of God's forgiveness. He went on to say that we must then turn from our sinful ways, repent! He then said that if we were ready to do that, then we must simply accept that Jesus is who He says He is, the Son of God, and accept Him and His redemptive work into our hearts. This preacher knew exactly what we needed to do, and I was eager to profess all of these things to this Jesus that had given me a new heart. The preacher led us in a prayer so that we could confess these things with our mouths.

When the preacher welcomed me into the family of God, I stood aghast as I asked, "What has happened to me?"

The preacher smiled knowingly and replied, "My dear, no doubt about it, you are Born Again."

I made my way back to my seat and saw life with new eyes. Everything was new and different. I knew, because I knew, because I knew, that indeed, I was born again.

20

The people and especially my friend, Estelle, were saying, "Hallelujah," so I said, "Hallelujah," and have never stopped saying it.

That very night I was marveling at the events of the day and decided to pour myself a whiskey, straight on the rocks as was my custom. I lifted the beautiful cut glass goblet, holding the whiskey as if in a toast to God. As I did this, the glass smashed into hundreds of pieces and the whiskey fell all over my skirt. That shook me up considerably as I realized that this day had been different from any other in my life and that if I were to embrace a new life, whiskey would not be a part of that life.

Dazed, I found a cigarette and lit up. But, instead of enjoying smoking as I had done for years, the cigarette tasted positively foul in my mouth. That was the last cigarette I smoked to this day.

Things were changing at an extremely fast rate in my life. God was cutting to the quick, and things of my old nature were falling away rapidly. I was a new creation, that was so clear, but even my eyes had a new fire in them. I could see it. God was changing me from the inside out. *"Therefore, if anyone is in Christ, he is a new creation; old things have passed away; behold, all things have become new."* 2 Cor 5:17.

In twelve hours time there seemed to be a complete change in my nature and I had new purpose for my life. My old desires had begun to fade away already. Somehow, at this early age in my new life I knew that this had everything to do with Jesus, but I knew too, for me, it had a lot to do with the country of Israel.

In this incredibly short time I had been delivered from alcohol, from smoking, and had been directed towards my destiny, Israel.

The next day I rushed out to tell all my friends how I was born again and suddenly, every single so called friend turned away from me. I was alone for the first time in my life. But was I really alone? Indeed not, Jesus was leading me, living in me, and the same joy that I had seen in my precious Estelle now was mine.

I was born again, and from that day until now I haven't stopped praising God for blessing me the way He has. Living in adventure with Jesus has and continues to surpass all my hopes and dreams for a life worth living, because I'm serving the giver of life, the lover of my soul. Hallelujah!

Because I had been a heavy all rounder. Heavy smoker, drinker, and party-goer. These excesses eventually triggered my childhood chest weaknesses, and asthma reared its ugly head. Still, the Lord had done such a marvelous job of meeting me where I was, so I was confident that He would also correct my asthma problem. I had tried on numerous occasions to break the disease myself, and never could. If I became unduly upset about anything I would start to wheeze, and within a very short time I would be unable to speak as my face swelled, and my windpipe closed.

How well I remember the times I was taken to the hospital and immediately injected with cortisone to relieve my distress. I was always exhausted afterwards, as my body tried to right itself of the trauma of not being able to breathe. For less severe attacks I carried an atomizer of cortisone with me, and had been advised to never be without it. I suffered from a self-inflicted disease, but I couldn't conquer it by my own will.

Naturally I yearned for good health, and when studying my Bible, I tried applying everything to my life, while concentrating on the healing scriptures. My faith was growing in leaps and bounds, and the day came when I decided that God was sufficient in all situations; and by faith I had actually been healed 2000 years ago on the cross as Jesus took the sin and suffering of humanity on his own body, so that those who believed in Him would be free.

The revelation of this truth was profound. I reasoned therefore God must still have His hand on me; and *"with God all things are possible,"* Mark 10:27. Once again an immediate metamorphosis took place, as I experienced a mind-blowing conversion in the area of health. I felt like a totally new person; a different person. I experienced such joy and exhilaration! It was like a window had opened in the sky, and I had seen "something." I caught a glimpse of another world, another existence with purpose and satisfaction. My former life seemed shallow and meaningless. It was a cataclysmic event. Somehow I had witnessed the meaning of life. My encounter was so intense that it called for extreme action. I sincerely felt that I was healed; so on that day I threw away my medication and atomizer, and that was that.

Everyone I saw afterwards was a target for my message, which was that I had been healed by the stripes of Jesus. This often required an additional explanation, which led to further witnessing of the greatness and goodness of God.

I sailed along buoyantly for about ten days. Then I bumped into an old friend in town. She had heard about my conversion and was very interested to hear how it had all come about. I was delighted to tell all.

"Do you still suffer from asthma?" She enquired.

"Oh no," I went on to tell her excitedly, "the Lord has healed me!" As I said these words, I immediately felt a definite catch in my breathing and that dreaded fear of the closing of the windpipe. My friend, a Nursing Sister, realized, as I did, what was happening, and we stood there staring at each other. I was about to have a lesson on "standing your ground," but since I had never had such a lesson, I did not know what to do. It was a scary moment.

"You need medication, and quickly!" said, my friend, as she steered me towards a pharmacy. I walked somewhat reluctantly, trying to grasp what was happening. At the door of the pharmacy a real spiritual tug-of-war began with my thinking and emotions, not to mention with my friend, who was quite anxious by this stage. I felt the Lord saying to me, "If you ask for medication you will lose the healing I have given you." At the same moment, fear gripped my heart as I dreaded the thought of being unable to breathe, and knew the doctors had told me time and time again, that if I didn't have my medication at a time such as this I could die.

By now my very concerned friend, was pulling on my arm as she read all the medical symptoms on my face. Although it takes some time to write down what happened, my decision was made in a split second in time. The question facing me was whether or not I believed in my divine healing.

"If you trust and believe in me," I felt the Lord impress upon me, "Walk away from the pharmacy, and the healing will be yours forever. If you enter the pharmacy and obtain the medication you think you need, you will have undone the work I have accomplished in your life. The choice is yours, Maureen. Which do you choose?"

With not a moment's hesitation I physically disentangled myself from my friend's grasp and ran as fast as my shaking legs could carry me. Every step away from the pharmacy brought an improvement in my breathing. I ran further and faster, with joy welling up in my heart, in sheer victory. I had made my choice, God had honored it, and from that day to this I am truly healed.

I don't want to give the impression that I am impervious to sickness. I'm not. God is not a magic formula for cures. Some people are never cured. I believe that sometimes illness strikes to slow us down; and I have the greatest respect for the medical profession. God has chosen many doctors to carry on His healing with the skill and knowledge available to them.

I believe though, that the plan God has for each and every one of our lives is the plan of destiny; and it only comes into being with the Born Again experience. His plan is higher and more wonderful than any human can imagine. After all, you are now His, and he knows far better than you do yourself, what is best for you. When your race is eventually run, and all is said and done, I believe that the only regret those of us who have faithfully served the Lord with our lives will have, is that we did not know Him, and serve Him sooner. After all, He is the giver of life, the lover of our soul.

Reviewing my own life as I relate these events, I see that I could easily have died as a child. When I was 22, I was the victim of a dreadful motor accident, which resulted in me not being able to walk for two years. However, I have amazing tenacity to live; and courage to overcome; attributes which I believe were given to me by God. Many times in my life I could have been taken away in that pine box, but I knew God was with me, and always will be for everyone who trusts in Him through all their trials and tribulations throughout life, until we complete the task for which we were born. That task being to become a soldier for Christ, and to do exploits in His name, and for His purpose; blood-washed children of God; living holy lives, in the world but not of it. In other words, existing for a divine purpose.

When that task is done, and we are no more to be found on this dusty earth, we shall be forever in the presence of God; with all those of like mind, redeemed from the earth for reasons and purposes far higher than we could ever realize or understand.

Chapter 3

I Work In A Yeshiva

Written by: Maureen Williamson

An American sister in Christ found herself sitting next to a well-known Israeli Rabbi on a flight bound for New York. They enjoyed each other's company, and high up in the skies, during the course of the conversation, the Rabbi told my friend that he was looking for an English-speaking secretary. His previous secretary a Jewish lady from Africa, had been exceptional. However, she had returned to her country, and he needed a replacement. My friend, Cora Jo, happened to mention that she knew of someone who, strangely enough, was also from Africa. The person she was speaking about, of course, was me.

"Ah well, I won't be back in Jerusalem for another six weeks," said the Rabbi. "

"I myself will not return there for a couple of months." rejoined Cora Jo. However, being the woman of faith that she is, she added, "if it is God's will, the position will be available. Let's wait and see what happens." Cora Jo and the Rabbi didn't even think to exchange telephone numbers.

Sometime later, when both the Rabbi and Cora Jo were back in Jerusalem, they walked around a busy corner in the center of the city, and bumped right into each other! As they regained their composure, they recognized one another and laughingly, the Rabbi enquired whether, by any chance, that secretary whom they had discussed some months back might still be available. Cora Jo said, "Yes, she is." With a broad smile she said, "It must be God's will that you interview her!"

I received the message that afternoon, and that same day, found myself sitting all bright-eyed and bushy-tailed, in front of the Rabbi. Nothing at that moment could have thrilled me more than the prospect of working for a Rabbi at a Jewish Yeshiva. (The Yeshiva is a training college where Jewish men study the Torah [Law] as well as the Talmud [a collection of ancient writings on Jewish civil and ceremonial law and tradition], and other Rabbinical writings.)

The Rabbi was a tall, ominous looking man, with an extremely serious expression on his face. His shoulder-length ringlets falling over the shoulders of his somber black suit denoted religious sobriety. There was an air of authority about him that said, "Don't bother me, as I'm about very important business." He was obviously a very perceptive man as well, who had a sixth sense about me, as his first words to me were, "You're a born-again Christian, aren't you?"

"Hallelujah, that I am." I replied.

"That Is exactly what concerns me," he said.

"I would consider it a privilege to work amongst you and the students," I said, "and I am a good secretary."

"You're a little too confident for my liking," said the Rabbi.

"I thought that was a good thing." Was my smiling reply. He studied my face for a while, then he said, "No, I don't think you are suitable."

"Sure I'm suitable. Give me a chance, and you will see," I said.

"I can see in your face that you are a missionary, and that frightens me." Declared the Rabbi.

"I am a missionary. What more can I say? I am committed to the truth."

He smiled and said, "There you are, you just said it. You definitely won't do."

I sat forward in my seat, and as nicely as I could, I said, "I will do Rabbi. I will do very well. I not only want the job, but I need it. What's more, I give you my word that I will not speak of my faith whilst I am on duty."

The Rabbi laughed. "I don't believe you can promise that as every inch of you oozes your commitment to Jesus Christ. How can you even make a promise like that?"

"Give me a chance, Rabbi." I said, with a sort of merry twinkle in my eye that was taken as a wink by the Rabbi.

"And now you have winked at me," said the Rabbi blushing. "Whatever am I to do with you?"

"Employ me," I replied. And we laughed together.

"I will hold you to your promise." Said the Rabbi. "Be here at 8:00 A.M. sharp tomorrow."

I was about to kiss him, but decided that would not be a wise move. "Yes Rabbi, I'll see you in the morning." We didn't even discuss salary. I was just so pleased that I was going to mix with these people, that nothing else really mattered.

The next morning, when I reported for duty wearing my pretty clothes, and my specially made up face, the looks I received from everyone were astounding. You'd think they'd never seen a woman before. Perhaps I'd better explain that orthodox Jewish women do not consider makeup a normal part of daily life. The woman's role in a religious Jewish setting in present day Israel is an unpretentious one. The ladies are always extremely plain, even drab in appearance. She is highly honored by her husband and children, and her function is to create and keep an atmosphere of Jewishness in the home. She is known for her piety, soberness and modesty, not to mention her effectiveness in keeping a kosher home.

My decision was firm. I would not share the Gospel, so I would have to approach the people differently, and this would be the hard part. My life would have to do the talking. It turned out that I was secretary to a number of the junior Rabbis as well. Each one came to me in fear and trepidation, telling me what they required of me in a secretarial capacity, but not one of them could look me in the eye. I was so ignorant of Jewish culture that I broke every rule in their book. I touched them, smiled at them, and stared at them till they responded. It was gloriously amusing, because as much as they all liked me, I was foreign, and therefore unpredictable, and possibly even dangerous. Still, I could clearly tell that I had won a place in their hearts, and that was my objective. Hallelujah!

I was in my element, mingling ever so unorthodoxly amongst these very orthodox people. My promise was an extremely difficult one to keep, nevertheless, keep it I did, by biting my lip. When I left the office, my promise no longer held. So after hours, I made up for lost time. All in all, it was quite a workable agreement. The Senior Rabbi, who had conducted the interview with me, was watching me very carefully .....and I was watching him! The status quo continued for several months.

The working week was over, and I had agreed to meet a friend in town. I walked from the Old City to the New, and waited at our prearranged rendezvous; a tiny park in the center of town. I sat down on one of the benches provided. My friend had not yet arrived, so while I waited I read the New Testament which I always carry around with me. There were six or more benches in the park and only two were occupied. Out of the corner of my eye I noticed a young Jewish girl walk through the park, look around, and then headed for the bench where I was sitting. We smiled at each other, and she pulled out a copy of the Old Testament. The Old and the New an the same bench!

As I would normally do, I greeted her, told her my name, and within moments we were engaged in conversation. Hava and I were both women of faith, so that is where the conversation remained. As I told her of my love for Jesus Christ, and my purpose in coming to Israel, her eyes grew larger and larger. When I related that I had recently been employed at a well-known Yeshiva as the Rabbi's secretary, she could not contain herself any longer.

"How is it possible that you are in a position like that, believing as you do?"

"All things are possible with God." I replied. Both of us agreed on that point.

My friend whom I had arranged to meet did not arrive; and an hour later the interesting young Jewish girl and myself were still deep in conversation on the same topic. It was the eve of the Shabbat, and my new companion invited me to come home with her, to meet her mother and father. I accepted her gracious invitation with delight, never realizing what the future would hold from this innocent encounter.

I knew Hava came from an Orthodox family, as her appearance was very plain. Her dress was long, dull and unflattering, her face devoid of make-up and a scarf covered her crowning glory. Her parents dressed in the same manner. I was made very welcome in their tiny home, and I answered all their questions, and freely shared the Gospel with them.

I knew I was swimming against the current along which their lives normally flowed, but that's my nature I'm afraid. After all, I had come to Israel for that very purpose; believing the Gospel needed to be shared with the Jew first, and then the rest of the people, to the utmost corners of the earth. Very little intimidates Maureen, and I found this to be my greatest tool in regard to evangelism in Israel, or indeed anywhere else in the world for that matter.

We shared the Shabbat meal together, and I left, believing that I had made some charming new friends whom I hoped to see again. Of course, things are not always as they seem, and I was about to discover the cost of sharing the Gospel with Hava and her family.

Sunday is a working day in Israel, and I set off rejoicing in the goodness of God, as I made my way to the Yeshiva. On entering the building I noticed the Rabbi waiting for me. Taking my arm he steered me into his office. I could see by the look on his face that things were not as they should be. My mind was running in circles. Why was he treating me this way? I was very confused by his strange behavior, as I knew I had kept my promise to him, so what could possibly be wrong? Sitting in the Rabbi's office were two very foreboding looking Jewish gentlemen, dressed in Orthodox garb, and looking even more troubled than the Rabbi. In an attempt to lighten the heavy atmosphere, I cheerfully greeted them in Hebrew; but the greeting fell on deaf ears. I was shown to a chair, and found myself almost an object of curiosity, as all three gentlemen stared hard at me for a long time. All I could do was stare back, feeling decidedly peculiar.

Finally the Rabbi introduced the two gentlemen as Officers from the Department of Religious Affairs. I felt myself jump a little. With a finger pointed at me in an intimidating fashion, one of them finally spoke. "We have come to inform you, in case you did not know, that the State of Israel is against missionaries. We are a Jewish State you know."

"As if I didn't know." I muttered to myself.

"Are you, or are you not, a missionary!" He asked accusingly, with his finger still pointing, and his face a strange shade of red.

"I am an Ambassador and Disciple of Jesus Christ, and if that is what you call a missionary, then I guess I am a missionary."

His finger stopped pointing, and his face seemed to cool down at my admission, as he went on to tell me that Hava and her parents had lodged an official complaint against me. "You are fired, as of now." I was told, as they nodded to the Rabbi. "With the evidence we have of your meeting with this family, we have every right to deport you; barring you from ever returning to Israel."

Now it was my turn to feel my face change color, not to red, but to white. There was nothing I could say to defend myself in their hands, I could see that they held a record of my words from the previous Shabbat. There wasn't one syllable I could have retracted, so only God could be my judge.

"You may go." They said, dismissing me with a wave of the hand. We advise you to leave Israel willingly, before another similar charge is filed against you."

I said, "I have spoken nothing but the truth, so help me God." My face streamed with tears.

My pay packet was waiting on my desk as I went to clear my few belongings. I left without another word, sad to be leaving, but glad that God had given me such favor amongst a select group of people that few Christians ever have a chance to speak to, let alone have contact with. But the gospel is an offence to the unsaved man who refuses to hear the truth. As I walked away my tears dried. I knew in my heart of hearts that God was pleased with me. I had accomplished my purpose there. I also knew that I would speak at the very next opportunity. So, instead of feeling depressed, I actually felt elated. Scripture was ringing in my heart and ears, and there was no sadness in me. Count it all joy, the Lord told us, if we are persecuted for His Name's sake. *"This know also, that in the last days perilous times shall come."* 2 Tim 3:1. *"Therefore I take pleasure in infirmities, in reproaches, in necessities, in persecutions, in distresses for Christ's sake: for when I am weak, then am I strong."* 2 Cor 12:10.

No wonder I was placed there, amongst those scholars of the Talmud and Jewish Law; at the very seat of the Jewish religion. Did my lifestyle and attitudes really reveal their Messiah, along with all their studying? Only the Holy Spirit can convict man. Only the One who sits upon the throne, Yeshua haMashiach, (Jesus Christ), can set a man free from the bonds of sin and religion. I believe that one day, fruit will be borne from the experiences of the Yeshiva, but only He knows exactly when and how.

I never saw Hava or her parents again, but it really was a case of history repeating itself, as I, like Paul, was persecuted for His Name's sake. My few months at the Yeshiva were invaluable, and I will never forget them.

As it turned out I wasn't deported, I left of my own accord. I returned again to Israel, and will most probably continue in this way for as long as I have breath in my body, for my love goes out to the Jewish nation from whence came my precious Messiah.

(Names have been altered to protect the privacy of the young girl.)

Chapter 4

A Golden Opportunity

Written by: Maureen Williamson

What a glorious feeling one gets from giving ... giving anything. The greater the giving, the greater the joy. Those who have
learned this Godly principle can get quite intoxicated by their
actions. Usually you can recognize the givers by the smiles on
their faces, and the quality of their joy. But nobody can out-give
God, the giver of Life, who frees us in turn to give.

In the natural realm, there are laws attached to gravity and
electricity. So too, in the realm of the Spirit there are laws attached
to giving. Yet how few understand these laws and choose to operate in this manner, bringing benefit to all concerned.

All the givers that I have been privileged to meet are in a class of their own. They have found and used the key that unlocks the door to true happiness.

A "giving" person whom I had never met, but who obviously knew of me, used to make a regular deposit of Bibles in a plain, brown package on my doorstep. They were written in the three major languages used in Israel, (Hebrew, Arabic, and English), and I received them with delight, making a point of distributing them as quickly as possible.

At the risk of death, the Bibles carry life .....

To be able to give God's Word to a living soul is a wonderful and joyous act. Think for a moment of countries where people are denied this advantage. They are satisfied even to be able to share one page at a time. They memorize the Word, and invariably are stronger and more effective, because the Word is hidden, buried deep within their hearts. Reflect too, for another moment, on the dedicated believers who smuggle Bibles into these countries. At the risk of death they carry life.

Bible distribution is always exciting. The reactions of those receiving is never the same. Whether they accept or reject the Word is not the issue. As Christians we are commissioned to carry the Gospel to a dying world, and that world is wherever we find ourselves living and stationed.

You'd be hard pressed to come by a more radical company of people than the one I was in. That's how I would describe the group that I became involved with. All shapes and sizes, all ages and backgrounds, but literally impregnated with the power to overcome. Giving Bibles is true giving; the giving of ourselves, a small token of our appreciation of what we realize has been given to us. What an incredible thing it is to be able to be coworkers with Christ, using all we have at our disposal to touch the lives of a lost and dying world.

It's strange that there is a stigma attached to giving Bibles, when it's the truth being given. The study of this truth is guaranteed to change the life of the reader. Perhaps this is the very reason for the stigma. Too many people are satisfied with their lives, and would rather stay just the way they are. To change their minds is a risk, and risk equals danger. However, risk, when based on God's Word, is not risk at all. It is God's formula for natural and exciting living.

We were mingling with the crowds of people all the time, trying to ascertain which language each one was speaking. We spoke to them in the degree to which they allowed us. Bibles were being handed out left, right and center. Suddenly, somebody exclaimed, "Watch out, here comes the President!" The group dispersed, and I found myself close to the cavalcade of security authorities, and Israeli strong-armed personnel. The kind which usually surround a Head of State.

Excitement welled up within me as I threw all caution to the wind. I wasn't going to let an opportunity like this pass me by. I did a little skip, and feeling my cheeks burning with enthusiasm, I bounced up through the officials. Instead of restraining me, they actually smiled and made a path for me to walk right up in front of the President of Israel. It was a never to be forgotten moment of exhilaration - the pure thrill of seizing a golden moment.

"Hello, Mr. President," I said. He gulped in astonishment, and stared at his security men in disbelief.

"It's okay sir," I said. "All I want to do is give you a precious gift. The greatest gift in the world. You do want the answers to the world's problems, don't you?"

He relaxed, laughed, and replied, "of course I do!"

"Well," I said, handing him a Bible. "Here it is, Mr. President!"

At that point, somebody stepped forward as if to remove me. The President motioned to him that it was OK, and putting his arm around my shoulders, he squeezed me, and said most graciously, "Thank you. I really need this."

With that, I walked confidently through the security men with a smile on my face, and disappeared into the crowd.

Truly it is more joyous to give, than to receive. We are exhorted to do so by ever increasing measures. When we are obedient to this work, we are often pleasantly surprised by the results!

Chapter 5

An Oasis Called Cyprus

Written by: Maureen Williamson

I stood at Ben Gurion International Airport in Tel Aviv with the same little green suitcase at my side with which I had come to Israel seven years before. I had that same feeling of expectancy, but now I was going in the opposite direction back to my home country, Zimbabwe, in Africa.

Having traveled so much I have no problem with a new location. The Kingdom of God is within us, so we take this wherever we go. It is sad to think that some people imagine it is a geographical location and therefore they only operate with effectiveness and enthusiasm when they are in a particular place. The Lord clearly told us; *"Every place that the sole of your foot shall tread upon, that have I given unto you, as I said unto Moses."* Joshua 1:3.

An expectant attitude, and a real love for God are the two basic requirements in serving Him. It's not a matter of "who you know," but rather "whose you are."

My parents had arranged a pre-paid ticket; the first portion of which I was able to collect in Israel. The African portion of the ticket would be held for me at the Air Zimbabwe check-in counter at Larnaca, Cyprus International Airport. The flight to Cyprus from Israel, which normally takes less than an hour, was now delayed almost three hours due to some unheard of malfunction of the landing gear. Finally the problem was sorted out, and we took off.

I watched Israel's coastline, now bathed in the rays and long shadows of the setting sun, disappear below us and thought to myself, "what will tomorrow bring?" I felt as though a glorious chapter of my life was closing, but what I was about to enter into surely would be just as glorious. The Lord always adds to, and does not desire to take away from us except that which is harmful to us in some way.

I had come to learn over the years that the joy of living one day at a time has many advantages. I believe there is no pattern of life more exciting. When I began I never realized that in following Christ it would be required of me to forsake everything of this world's "system." At that time I don't think this prospect would have appealed to me. However, it certainly does now, as I am not reliant on anyone, or anything other than God's glorious Word, which totally sustains me. I have come to the place where I am unable to be bought or sold with things of this world. My life has been bought with the great price of Jesus on the cross.

My walk of faith, casting all caution to the wind, has borne real fruit and an assurance that God's Word never fails. As long as we continue to seek His Kingdom, everything else shall be added unto us. Jesus was a radical, and His followers, by virtue of His message, are the same. It is human nature to wonder about the future, and I know many Christians who seem to spend all their waking hours imagining events to come. The future is tomorrow, and will unfold in its perfect time. It is far more productive and meaningful to live this day to its fullest, and in so doing, you will live tomorrow in the same manner too.

How can the product of our puny human imaginations compare with what God has in store *"And we know that all things work together for good to them that love God, to them who are the called according to his purpose."* Romans 8:28. Surely He is the God who invented adventure, variety and excitement! I believe it all revolves around how we perceive God, and how certain we are that He loves us. If we have really understood the price that Jesus has paid for us at Calvary, we would be convinced that He will withhold nothing good from us. He has a tailor-made plan for our lives.

Is He involved in all aspects of our lives, both major and minor, or just there in times of crisis, when we have exhausted our own understanding? Scripture proves the former is correct. He is involved in every aspect, and in everything that happens to us, and will ultimately bring good from all of it. Revelation 3:20 says, *"Behold, I stand at the door, and knock: if any man hear my voice, and open the door, I will come in to him, and will sup with him, and he with me."* He will not enter unless He is invited. This also refers to the circumstances of our lives, inclusive of future plans and ambitions. Once we willingly relinquish our own hold upon our lives, God steps in with His plan, exceedingly above and beyond our expectations.

Allow me to illustrate.... Here I am on my way to Africa, yet again. This trip is different however. My dear old dad had suffered a couple of strokes, and as a result was quite incapacitated. My mother was well and active, but tired, which was understandable at 80 years of age. After much prayer and consideration on my part, coupled with a cry for help from my parents in Zimbabwe, I decided that I should go home to be with them.

Having had my own home, being single and independent for ten years, it was not an easy decision to make. My life in Jerusalem, my possessions, my precious friends, my responsibilities, my commitments, everything that I held dear and valuable I would have to walk away from. I knew that I could not just go to my parents for a short while. This was God's timing, and I understood that, *"Behold, to obey is better than sacrifice."* 1 Samuel 15:22.

As Christians we are called to lay everything of our lives on the altar and that includes possessions, emotions, and all our desires. We are to be willing to walk away from that altar at any given moment and leave those things behind trusting that the God who provided them can do so again. But, there are times when this is easier to preach than walk it out, and this was one of those times.

I was leaving Jerusalem, not knowing if I would ever return. I had wrestled with my conscience for a few months, as it was a painful decision. Years ago I had wrestled with the once for all, 'Yes, Lord.' Meaning that for anything my Lord asked me to do, I would simply say, 'Yes, Lord.' Sooner or later though, everybody has to face a situation where we consider a 'No, Lord.' These are critical answers and can affect us all the days of their lives. As a faithful Christian, I want to be, and believe I am being led by the Lord on a daily basis. As I yielded once again to His Spirit within me, I managed another, 'Yes, Lord.'

It was interesting to hear the reactions from my friends. Most people are very set in their ways, and some of my pals are the same. "How can you leave everything, and go off to Africa? How can you just pack up, leave your friends, your flat, etc., etc.? " They were horrified that I wanted to break out of "the mold," and move away from what was considered the norm. The lack of security terrified them. To them, a routine was what constituted a "secure life." Daring to do something a little different was unthinkable.

Certainly, no two people view issues in the same way. Still, there is only one way, and that is the right way. Words are cheap. Action is what counts. The crux of the matter is that God's will is done in our lives. The fact is that we need to know how God views every issue of our lives. Our friends, no matter how dear they may be to us, do not stand in our shoes, and ultimately are not responsible for our choices. We alone are answerable for our own decisions and shall bear the consequences of them.

With the one hour Air Cyprus flight nearly over our plane approached the Island of Cyprus. Larnaca lay straight ahead. Although there appeared to be only darkness outside my window, I knew that tomorrow would reveal a shimmering Mediterranean Sea washing upon long pebbly beaches. The red roofs and white stucco buildings sporting geranium filled window boxes would stand out in the morning sunlight. In the distance would be the shadowy form of the Troodos Mountains looming far above the glimmering sea shores.

Soon I was off the plane and more drama was to unfold as I appeared at the ticket counter. I was distressed to discover that the ticket for the final leg of the trip was nowhere to be found, and nobody knew anything about it!

Throughout the flight from Tel Aviv I had been concerned about the short connection time due to the delay in Israel. I had even alerted the flight attendants on the plane. They had radioed ahead to Larnaca to have my boarding pass ready. The attendants had ushered me quickly from the plane ahead of the other passengers.

I stood there in amazement as I heard the final boarding call of my Air Zimbabwe flight announced, and the plane taxied toward the runway. Moments later it was pointed steeply into the air leaving Cyprus behind. That was the flight I was supposed to be on and it took off without me.

I knew Air Zimbabwe only flew from Cyprus once a week. I also knew I had no money, nor winter clothing, except what I was wearing. I had sold my entire winter wardrobe in Israel, since I was flying to Africa where substantial winters don't really exist. I know people in most places in the world, but Cyprus wasn't one of them. I smiled and said, "Here I am Lord .... help!"

My being there caused quite an incident. At this time in history carrying a South African Passport did not guarantee trouble free processing through International Airports. My Passport was quickly taken away, and would only be made available to me on my departure. The ticket officer was embarrassed because of the inexplicable confusion with my ticket, which was eventually traced to another agent on the opposite side of the island.

Normally Air Cyprus would have been responsible since their delay had caused all these complications. Nevertheless when they found out that it wasn't entirely their fault, they conveniently stepped out of the picture!

So there I was, virtually penniless, stranded in Cyprus.

My thoughts went back to Israel...

Not long ago I had finished writing my first book, 'Audacity To Love.' The printing costs were astronomical, and rising all the time. It was a leap of faith to imagine that in my last month in Israel, everything would come together. To make up the balance of what was owing, I sold everything I had in the world. Instead of

46

having a few scattered, moldy possessions, I put every cent into the book and with great joy, two weeks before my day of departure, there in front of me in book form, was my life for the past couple of years. It was a good trade. Who can compare "things" with "experiences" after all?

Looking around the ticket counter, I couldn't help but notice one of the Air Cyprus personnel, a good-looking Greek, taking an interest in my problem. All conversations were conducted in the Greek language, which left me somewhat out on a limb. It was nearing midnight when this same handsome young man walked up to me with his hand extended, and a beautiful smile on his face.

"I am going to take care of you. Come this way please. You must be hungry, I would like to take you to dinner." Not another word was spoken, and we simply walked away together.

I know it could have been dangerous, disappearing into the night with a complete stranger. He could have been somebody with connections in the underworld of gangsters and drug barons.... but my instincts told me to trust him.

We sat together in a romantic candle-lit restaurant until the early hours of the morning. My Greek brother was a beautiful Christian gentleman, whom the Lord had sent to help this sister in distress. He booked me into a most delightful little hotel on the waterfront, which was run by another member of his family, and proceeded to pay for my bed and breakfast for one week.

At this point I want to state a caution here. One must be so very sensitive to the Holy Spirit. It is not OK to just walk off into the night with any handsome man that offers help. I've rejected many such offers in my Christian life. This was an extreme exception and I knew the Lord had engineered this entire situation and was simply providing for my needs.

I accepted this gift most graciously and thankfully. The following day he flew off to London on business. Can you see God's provision for His people?

I found it was wonderful to catch my breath and enjoy lovely walks all over that beautiful island. I wore my shoes out walking here, there, and everywhere. I encountered many local Cypriot people still living an ancient lifestyle and speaking their native tongue, Greek. They were plainly dressed and noticeably rough from a hard work ethic. Heavily laden donkeys carried produce and a variety of wares to market in the large hand woven baskets made especially for the animal. Lively Greek music could often be heard coming from shops and houses. Distinctive aromas of the Middle Eastern Greek foods filled the air.

There are times in our lives when we need to pull away from all activity to be refreshed. God in all His wisdom knew that my very full life in Israel had worn on me, and that the time ahead with my parents would be also very taxing. A week long break in this oasis called, Cyprus was the breather I needed between two radically different lifestyles.

While drawing away from the world, I also found myself on an enforced "fast." Even this I took as from the Lord, as I easily survived on the simple breakfast provided with my room. Each morning to start my day I trooped down the single flight of stairs to the lobby where a glass of orange juice, a slice of toast, and coffee awaited me. That would be my daily banquet for six days! Fasting and not concentrating on the physical, the spiritual is able to be strengthened; thereby bringing us closer to the Lord.

One week later, Air Zimbabwe flew back to Cyprus, and it wasn't long before I was winging my way to Africa. I had lived one day at a time, and survived! Not only survived, but was thoroughly refreshed by a week created by God himself for my benefit.

Chapter 6

My African Roots

Written by: Maureen Williamson

My connecting flight to Bulawayo from Johannesburg, South Africa arrived on time, and I traveled the eight miles into the city by shuttle bus. The remaining two miles home were by Zimbabwe mini-taxi, not known for it's comfort, or space. The blazing African sun, high in the radiant blue sky, was my only welcome, as I stepped from the taxi in front of the home where I had been born.

Roses bloomed profusely along the driveway, but our exquisite garden was not so beautiful as it once was. It had been the pride of Bulawayo, winning house and garden awards when I was a child. Growing up in Bulawayo, I had imagined that everybody had a garden such as ours. I later traveled the world and found, in fact very few lived in the beautiful surroundings I was accustomed to.

There was no one to greet me, and this may have been indicative of the atmosphere I would encounter throughout my stay. I found Mom and Dad in their bedroom, Dad upon the bed, and Mom sitting with him. I was shocked to see how frail they were after an absence of only one year. They had aged drastically. It was a tearful reunion. Dad had been very upset and worried over the fact that I was delayed in Cyprus for an entire week when my connecting flight had been missed. I was penniless, and he had fretted deeply.

'Being penniless,' had not bothered me nearly as much as knowing my globe trotting days were on hold for a while. My lifestyle had become one of dependance and trust in my Lord, having no money was not a concern. I knew I would always have all that I needed to travel and serve my God. He was, and is, faithful in every way. But, this assignment would require quite an adjustment. I was committed to doing just that and knew my God would provide the grace and determination required. The Lord had shown me that I was to lay my life down in honor of my parents according to His commandment, (Exodus 20:12), in their final days on earth.

My Dad was no longer active, capable, nor interested in all things. He had always been very much in charge. He now just sat, looked into space, and relived life in his mind. Dad regretted that he had overlooked the important issues of life as his priority was to gain wealth. He achieved the wealth, but at the expense of relationships, and now he sat and thought about it incessantly. Still, where there is life, there is hope. It was not too late to build relationships, I kept reassuring my Dad.

My Mother, who was always subservient to my father, had undergone a huge change.

She had taken over Dad's role, and in doing so became quite a tyrant. This startled me and took every ounce of my patience and understanding to see the situation for what it really was. On my third day back home I was told to go to my room. It then occurred to me, even though I had lived independently in foreign lands for nearly twenty years, in the eyes of my parents, I remained their little girl.

On day four, my mother confronted me, asking why I had come back to Africa. Incredulous, I broke down. I tried to explain that they had asked me to please come and take care of them. Coupled with my understanding of God's Word, that was the reason I came back to Africa.

The stresses of living in confinement, after my foot loose and fancy free life, surmounted and I can truthfully say, those years were my most difficult and trying. They were full of opportunity to say, "Woe is me," but also full of lessons in life that reminded me, one day I would also be old and infirm. However, I knew if I was willing and obedient to do what God had set before me, no matter how repetitive and frustrating it was, I would be taken care of when my hour of need arrived.

Many times I was brought to my knees in prayer and tears, but at all times I heard the Lord say, "My grace is sufficient, press on." Each time this would strengthen me.

Praise God for the wonderful body of Christ in Africa. They took my tired arms and held them up when the weight became too much for me. Put under pressure, I was shocked to find I did not do so well, and cried all the more for God's grace. Time, I knew, was of the essence. I wanted above all else to know that when life was no more for my parents I would have an assurance of their eternal salvation. So with this objective always in mind, I found the strength to run the race.

There was no way of escape for me and I knew it would take more than myself to complete this task, and do it in love, which is the only way if our efforts are to please the Lord in the process. Often I was reminded by the Lord that my parents had given me life, and what I was doing was the least I could do to honor them. In honoring my parents, I honored God.

Months became years as I watched the process of decline, and in it all my parents were watching me and the principles of Christianity that I tried to uphold.

Overlooking human frustrations and the multiple anxieties of two people facing death without a real understanding of Jesus Christ was a scary experience, so I clung even closer to God's promise, *"Believe on the Lord Jesus Christ, and thou shalt be saved, and thy house."* (Acts 16:31).

The local Body of Christ came out of the woodwork to help in every way, and their ministry efforts were speaking loud and clear to my parents, who were confronted daily with a different kind of living, and loving. I watched in wonder and excitement as the Lord wooed both my parents into His glorious Kingdom, maybe late, but rather late than never. I enjoyed the privilege of leading both my parents in the same prayer of repentance, and acceptance of Jesus, as I had prayed twenty years before.

I had invested two long, hard years with my parents, but everything I experienced was worth it, and I have the assurance that I did what God required of me. The day came when I knew I was free to go again, and go I did, with a deep sense of satisfaction and joy that the mission was accomplished. A glorious eternity awaited my precious Mother and Dad.

In this African Roots experience I found out the best way of honoring God is to be a servant. I'm rejoicing to this day that I was sensitive to my parents call to come, even though at that time my life was most purposeful, most enjoyable, and fulfilling. God enabled me to serve in the higher purpose of my parents salvation.

I found out, as in the words of the saint, Corrie Tenboom, "The measure of life, after all, is not it's duration, but it's donation."

Chapter 7

Retrenchment

Written by: Maureen Williamson

Why does the word, 'retrenchment,' (or in the U.S., 'downsizing'), strike fear into everyone's heart? Why does it have such a paralyzing effect on anyone over 40 years of age in the business world? Perhaps it's because we live in a world where nothing is permanent; at least what used to be considered permanent twenty years ago, anyway.

Statistics show that the five most traumatic experiences known to man are: starting on the bottom of the ladder, retrenchment, moving house, bankruptcy, divorce, and at the top, the death of a loved one. Sometimes two of these calamities occur together.

The after-effects can be so crushing that some people never recover. And while one would never wish these on anyone, they are a part of life. Many people actually pull themselves up by their boot straps and improve their lives as a result.

Being retrenched had never been part of my life and I didn't want it to be, thank you very much. After all, I was so efficient, responsible, reliable, so excellent in every way. Who in their right mind would even consider dismissing me? When the rumblings of discontent started reverberating around the office I was unaffected. Then we discovered that ten of the staff of 150 were to get the chop. As the guillotine started to slide closer, the belief that I have of everything in life being cause and effect became very clear. I instinctively knew that if anything happened to me it would be the direct result of a certain young lady in the office who inadvertently loaded me with pressure, simply because she herself was in her own pressure cooker, and wanted some release in any form.

When the complaints swerved in my direction, and my marching orders were issued, I felt limp, devastated. Genevieve had very effectively taken the lid off and blasted me with her scalding steam.

Somewhere in the back of my head I had entertained this ridiculous idea that I would stay in this position till retirement; even though that was many years away. Now I felt 'washed up,' ' thrown on the heap'.... you know what I mean. My thoughts zeroed in on the lady who had caused my downfall. Those thoughts were far from kind, and I knew that no matter what, I had to deal with her. The question was how? I could be really mean and bear a grudge towards her, or I could be really smart and show her the gospel. I knew from past experience that there were only two courses of action, and the latter had always worked marvelously. I'd already lost everything in this situation, so I decided that my strategy would be to zap her with love; the love of God .... the most powerful force in the world. And so with my plan of action in place, I began to seek a new job. This was the time when things started to look very interesting.

First I prayed to God to fill my heart with love towards Genevieve, and for Him to prepare her heart to hear the Gospel. Almost immediately I lost all animosity towards her, and was able to return to being my usual bubbly self. My next step was to show friendship and care towards this woman who had cost me my job . This started off somewhat awkwardly, as it was so obvious, but I kept my silly grin on my face, and pressed on regardless. The following move took a little more persuasion on my part. I needed to get her to a church service. There was no stopping me now; a friendship had been formed, and we were really beginning to enjoy each other.

It wasn't long before the person sitting next to me in church was Genevieve. Her body movements revealed to me that she was more than just a little interested in what was going on too. My silly grin became a wide smile, and I watched in wonderment as Genevieve changed right before my very eyes. Not only her thinking, but her attitude, and even her appearance was dramatically different. I knew without a doubt that the next thing I would witness would be Genevieve Born Again.

In the midst of all this excitement I found a wonderful new job that was in every way an improvement on the old one. Everything was being made new; not only for Genevieve, but for me as well. God had in fact used this lady to improve my life. By this stage we were bosom buddies, and we both knew that we had been brought together by divine appointment for purposes far beyond what our human intelligence could comprehend.

A couple of weeks later, Genevieve, publically confessed Jesus as her Lord and Savior, and shortly afterwards was baptized in the same way that John the Baptist baptized Christ. She is born of the Spirit of God, born to walk where angels fear to tread, born to fulfill God's purposes on the earth.

Genevieve is living proof that once the Spirit of the Lord is within you, all things are made new in Christ. She has been transformed.

Welcome to all that God has for you my precious Sister.

Chapter 8

An Unexpected Blessing

Written by: Maureen Williamson

(A Jewish experience in Johannesburg)

I have this glorious friend, aptly named Gloria. She was born of a Jewish father, and there's no mistaking that unique Jewish look in her lovely face. The two of us were strolling through a fashionable Johannesburg shopping mall this particular day when suddenly two Jewish boys, who were clearly under ten years of age, materialized before our eyes. For some reason they zeroed in on me. Confronted by the older of the two boys, who were suitably attired for Sukkot, I was asked, "Are you Jewish?"

Don't ask me why, but I replied that I was. How amazing that I should say, "Yes," without a second thought. Perhaps I instinctively felt that I was. I love the people, honor the Old Testament, and somewhere inside me I think I am Jewish. My mannerisms certainly are, and I certainly have the chutzpah, (the audacity), to be Jewish.

I noticed the boys carried a palm branch, among other things, and the youngest lost no time in doing what he was there to do, as he gabbled in his excitement,

"Repeat after me." My heart leapt, and so did Gloria's, for we both intuitively knew that a blessing was about to be bestowed on us. The haunting music of the Hebrew language sprang from the young boy's lips, and there we were repeating each word. We had to say this, and do that, and then do and say something else, which involved a lot shaking of the items we had to hold.

Now the Sukkot, for those of you who don't know, is a time of rejoicing in the seasons, and an ingathering of the harvest crops. It starts on the 15th Tishrei, which is in the first month of the Jewish calendar. (See Leviticus chapter 23.)

Once the blessing had been pronounced we stood around smiling, with everybody happy. Only at this particular point did it occur to me that I needed to set the record straight. I held the young boy's hands and thanked him most sincerely for the blessing, and tried to explain the fact that I'm not really Jewish.

"I'm a righteous Gentile," I began.

The look of horror in the child's face was indescribable, as he stammered. "What can I do now? How can I take the blessing back?"

"You can't," I said. "Whenever you give a blessing you can't take it back. That's why a blessing is a blessing. And that's why my friend Gloria and I are so pleased that you came across our path today and may Hashem, (God), bless you too." We smiled as we waved goodbye.

I rushed home to study, in depth, what the Sukkot was really all about, and I found it fascinating indeed. All the shaking of the plants and the unusual fruit Gloria and I had been instructed to hold, was very important according to Jewish custom. It was necessary that we faced the East, towards Jerusalem, and the added shaking of the fruit symbolized Divine authority over all of creation.

The out of the ordinary fruit that Gloria and I were instructed to hold was an Etrog, (Citron). It resembled a large lemon, but was slightly heart-shaped, and the Old Testament states that an Etrog is required to be beautiful and free of blemishes. Even a minor defect may disqualify this fruit. It is regarded as a symbol of perfection. My research showed me that the specifications of this symbol were far stricter than those demanded of the other representations. Further reading revealed why this was so.

The Midrash, (legends pertaining to the Old Testament), states that the leaf of the myrtle branch is shaped like the eye, and its use in the Mitzvah of the four symbols indicates to us that we must direct our eyes towards the service of God, and not allow them to gaze upon things that would tempt us to sin. The myrtle has an aroma, but does not bear edible fruit. (The Mitzvah is a commandment of the Old Testament referring to all the "Do's" found in the Torah; "doing a good deed;" amounting to 613 in all. The Torah is the written and oral law. It is used more specifically in referring to the five books of Moses.)

The leaf of the willow branch has no fragrance and also does not bear fruit. It resembles the lips, teaching that we must guard our lips from speaking evil.

61

The palm, (Lulov), bears a delicious fruit but has no fragrance, and the branch is meant to be a dedication to fulfilling the Divine Will.

When the blessing over the four tokens is pronounced, it is the Etrog that is examined more closely. Apart from it needing to be without spot or blemish, as it is considered to be the most important of the four symbols, it is held alone in the left hand, apart from the other three plants, which are tied together, and held in the right. The Etrog is also pressed closely to the body so that it is near the heart, the most important organ of the body, where one's thoughts and feelings should be absorbed with sanctity.

Ideally, while sight, speech and deed should all be completely involved with holiness, a deviation from any of these areas may be considered to be an isolated phenomenon, not affecting the whole being. However, thoughts and feelings affect everything one does. The heart's devotion must therefore be complete; so a greater dedication is required that the heart be pure, possibly because it is considered the core of our creation.

Gloria and I had been fortunate enough, while in the City of Gold, to be part of a Jewish ceremony that had been passed down through the ages. We had truly been blessed.

Chapter 9

In You All The Families Of The Earth Will Be Blessed

Written by: Maureen Williamson

Christianity is so indebted to the Jewish teachings and prophets of old. Do we ever stop to thank them for preserving all that we value today? (Read Romans, chapter 11.) The apostle Paul tells us that we have a great spiritual responsibility to God's ancient Covenant people. That's why Christians are called to be peacemakers, summoned to be humble and sincere, and urged to show love and care. I would encourage you to open dialogue with a Jewish person. Learning about their history is an engrossing subject.

We should read the Old Testament, pray for Jewish people, and proclaim in love what their Messiah has done. *"And so, as those who have been chosen of God, holy and beloved, put on a heart of compassion, kindness, humility, gentleness and patience; bearing with one another, and forgiving each other, whoever has a complaint against anyone; just as the Lord forgave you, so also should you. And beyond all these things put on love, which is the perfect bond of unity. And let the peace of Christ rule in your hearts, to which indeed you were called in one body; and be thankful."* NAS, Colossians 3:12-15.

Paul tells us that Israel has experienced a hardening in part until the full number of the Gentiles has come in. *"And so all Israel will be saved, as it is written."* Romans 11: 26. And, *"the gifts and the calling of God are irrevocable."* Romans 11:29, NAS. And when the full number of the Gentiles has come into faith, and the Jewish people have embraced the Messiah, what then? Remember Jesus' lament in Luke 13:34-35? *"O Jerusalem, Jerusalem, Ye shall not see me, until the time come when ye shall say, Blessed is he that cometh in the name of the Lord."*

As we look forward with great expectation to the coming of our Messiah, let us make his paths straight by cherishing our Judaic roots and honoring the Jewish people. In this way we draw near to the reconciliation of the church and Israel that will hasten the return of the Messiah.

We approach ever more rapidly that day when Mark 14: 62 is fulfilled. Hallelujah! *"....ye shall see the Son of man sitting on the right hand of power, and coming in the clouds of heaven."*

Let us never forget that the true definition of a Jew is a Gentile brought into a peculiar relationship with God for the sake of world redemption. I fully believe that for this reason alone Israel is the apple of God's eye. God's plan of world redemption is vulnerable because of Israel's weakness, but it will nevertheless triumph because of God's faithfulness. Through Israel, God will sanctify His name in the nations throughout the earth.

It has been noted that God's plan of salvation is eternally planned before time, and exists beyond infinity. However, satisfaction can only come through faith in Jesus Christ, for Jews and Gentiles alike. By bequeathing of the land of Canaan to the Jewish people it is therefore also eternal. Or, as the Bible puts it, "everlasting." Israel, the land and the people, are crucial to the program of world redemption. Any attempt to destroy the Jewish people, or divest them from the land that God gave them originally, and for all time, is an attempt to frustrate God's plan of salvation.

Let's think about Abraham who became known as the friend of God. His is the only name which is venerated by Jew, Christian and Muslim alike. Their religions differ greatly, yet all revere Abraham, who was originally known as Abram, (Genesis 17:5). All claim equal relationship with the great patriarch, saying, "We have Abraham for our father."

Abraham turned his back on a life surrounded by pagans and idol worshipers, and became known as the "Friend of God." He listened and obeyed, leaving his home in Egypt, turning his back on his earlier false teachings to go out into the unknown without knowing where he was going, (Hebrews 11:9). However, he went willingly, because God had told him to go and he believed he was going under God's guidance. Remember that Abraham did not know about God as we do through the teachings of Jesus Christ. He only had dimly remembered teachings of Enoch, Methuselah and Noah. Ultimately Abraham became the trail blazer for his descendants though. He was a man who had begun to think.

Abraham thought about worshipful reverence, and couldn't comprehend how an animal or statue could command this. These were creatures or things that could be destroyed easily by man, so how could they be supreme? There is a Jewish teaching demonstrating that when man earnestly seeks God, really thinking deeply about Him, God can speak to make him hear, and man has the choice to listen and obey.

To none has the world owed so much, as it does to Abraham and his Jewish descendants. To them God committed His sacred revelations; and through the Savior all that was foretold has come to the world. To Abraham God revealed Himself as one who is righteous and who loves righteousness, and proved that He is willing to impart that righteousness to fallen mankind.

God asked a lot of Abraham. Abraham had to turn his back on everything he was familiar with, leaving family and country. It required discipline and courage. Would you be willing to agree to God's command to sacrifice your child, as Abraham did, with his son Isaac?

We should be committed to make ourselves acquainted with Israel's history; past, present and future, because earth's welfare is destined with it. Read your Old Testament. Paul tells us in his second letter to Timothy, *"All scripture is given by inspiration of God, and is profitable for doctrine, for reproof, for correction, for instruction in righteousness: That the man of God may be perfect, thoroughly furnished unto all good works."* 2 Timothy 3:16-17. *"All scripture!"* That includes the Old Testament. So there is no exception, either in our estimate of it, or the regard we pay to it. All alike claims our attention; all is given by the same authority ... God's?

Have you ever considered why the people of Israel are called "peculiar"? This is not to be derogatory in that they are odd; but rather that they are God's treasure; they are singular. Therefore the Hebrew nation, Israel's ancient and present day people remain God's treasure reserved for Himself forever.

The Jewish nation was called into existence by a supernatural act of God. Whether you like or dislike them won't make a scrap of difference. In other words, their origins are not like any other nation on this earth. We today can praise God that Abraham fully obeyed this supernatural call, as from him has come the entire Jewish nation. These people are the means by which God will reach the world, as God said to Abraham, *"and in thee shall all families of the earth be blessed,"* Genesis 12:3. The interpretation is confirmed in Matthew 1:2 and Luke 3:34.

GET EXCITED!! WE ARE ABOUT TO SEE THE FULFILLMENT OF ALL THAT WAS PROMISED.

Chapter 10

Taxi, Madam

Written by: Maureen Williamson

Going about my business on the busy streets of Jerusalem I always marvel at the electric blue, cloudless sky and at the activity, smells and sounds of this fascinating ancient city. The activity mostly consists of people pushing and shoving in a great hurry to get where they are headed. Few of them look beyond the next step. Only the daring look at peoples faces. They miss so much of interest by not being more observant, I think.

Not me! I do my best to look into the faces of the people and smile at anybody whose eye happens to catch mine. It's a small thing, a smile, but it can change someone's countenance immediately. Also it is said to be very good for the muscles in one's face. For these two reasons I smile a lot. Sometimes it gets me into trouble, but usually it doesn't.

I don't think God's face is stern and preoccupied. I picture God as smiling a lot, especially at the antics of some of us, His children.....

For those who have visited Jerusalem they will know that the streets are narrow and overcrowded with traffic and pedestrians, especially at peak times.

The Israeli's are somewhat short on patience and it's a fact that more people are killed and injured in road accidents than in twentieth century Israeli wars.

Taxi's seem to make up half the traffic. I often wondered what kind of a living taxi drivers make. Obviously quite a good one or else there wouldn't be so many around.

People in Jerusalem like to walk, so the taxi drivers move along and honk their horn at the next prospective customer, hoping they will decide to ride rather than walk. That's the life of the taxi driver in Jerusalem.

On this particular day this very cute Israeli drove his taxi alongside me, tooted his horn, tilted his head, smiled and said, "Taxi, Madam."

What a handsome specimen, I noticed immediately. I smiled back with a wave of my hand saying, "No thanks, but God bless you."

I looked back and noticed him watching me and I walked purposefully away.

A day or two later in a completely different part of Jerusalem, this same cute Israeli taxi driver again pulled up alongside me and said, "what about today? Where would you like to go, Madam?"

Again I said, "No thanks, but God bless you."

Over the next few weeks, and never in the same area, our paths crossed repeatedly. I actually started to look out for him, and obviously he was looking out for me also. Or maybe we are both just very observant people.

A few days later he again came alongside me with the honk of his horn and said, "My name is David, what is your name?"

This time I particularly noticed his beautiful dark brown eyes. I knew that both our hearts skipped a beat as I kept walking and called over my shoulder, "Hi, David. My name is Maureen."

I remember thinking, as I moved away and up the street, "I'd really like to talk to him about the Lord."

As I guess it was inevitable, after all Jerusalem is a small city, soon on another occasion I heard my name with a Hebrew accent being called from across the street. He was standing and this time waving earnestly like an old friend. He shouted across the street, "let's have coffee sometime, Maureen."

My heart skipped another little beat. I smiled saying, "maybe, God bless you," and went on my merry way.

I wondered about David. What else was he doing with his life besides following women around Jerusalem. I somehow knew he wasn't married and I certainly knew he liked me. He was Jewish for sure, and he was tall for an Israeli. He was athletic looking and probably played some sport. I wondered what his thinking was on Jesus Christ... I was certainly going to find out.

Sure enough, within a day or two there he was again. He drove alongside me and said, "Maureen, you've got something I want."

I laughed and so did he. "I'm Christian," I said, "and I take it very seriously."

"I can see that," David replied. "So when can we have coffee together? I really want to speak to you."

"What's the point," I asked? "I'm Christian."

"The point is, I want to get to know you," David said. "Please, Maureen, all I'm asking for is a cup of coffee." And his beautiful big brown eyes sparkled.

Feeling somewhat reckless, I said, "the next time you see me, OK, we'll go and have a cup of coffee.

"Be Met!" (Meaning, 'really!') "You promise."

"Be Met." I answered.

Well you guessed it, it wasn't even twenty-four hours later in another part of town on the way home from visiting a friend and David's taxi was alongside me once again.

"You promised, Maureen."

"I've got fifteen minutes."

"Met su Yan," ('excellent' in English), he replied.

I opened the door and got into the seat next to him.

David was so excited he reminded me of a child. He obviously didn't expect me to fulfill my word. I couldn't help but notice that his hands were shaking. "Why are you shaking," I asked.

"Why do you ask? Because I'm in love with you," David said.

I got such a shock I nearly jumped out of the taxi.

"From the first day I saw you, when you put your hand out towards me and said, 'God bless you', an arrow came out of your hand and went straight into my heart. And now I'm yours!"

"How positively ridiculous," I thought. But I could see by his expression that he was serious, and I marveled at the thinking of Middle Eastern men.

Five minutes later, holding my hand no less, he was telling me all about himself and his life. Indeed, he was younger than he looked. A baby in my eyes, at thirty-nine years old. Jewish and divorced with four young children that he spoke of with much love. He has eleven brothers. He loves and plays soccer. He is a Sabra, (born in Israel), and was raised in an Orthodox religious home and couldn't stand all the rules of religiosity. That is why he divorced. His parents are from Iraq and Iran, which makes him Kurdish Israeli. He made a real point of telling me that the Kurdish men are the best lovers in the world!

The fifteen minutes were soon up so I asked him innocently to drive me to my home.

"Sure," he said, "and now I know where you live. I must see you again, can I please have your phone number?"

I should have said, no you can't have the telephone number, and I shouldn't have let him know where I lived - but, anyway.......

The very next day David telephoned and said, "let's go out for a drive."

I said, "only if I can bring a chaperone." He didn't understand what that meant and when I explained it meant another person, he seemed disappointed. But, he reluctantly agreed.

I invited a girlfriend, a fellow believer, to accompany us and off we went zooming around Jerusalem in a taxi. We had fun together and I thought, "Great! David could be our new Israeli friend. He has lived in Jerusalem all his life and knew every inch of the city I love so much." And I reasoned, "the Lord must have brought him across my path for his salvation. Surely the Lord will give me the privilege of leading this cute beautiful brown eyed Israeli to Him....."

When we got back to my home I asked David to carry a rug which was too heavy for me to contend with. I had purchased it during our drive about the city. My friend went on to her own home.

My home is usually full of people, but on this occasion nobody was there. David put the rug down and the next thing I knew he kissed me like I've not been kissed for a long time.

Again I got the shock of my life. I tore myself away from his grasp, while David stared into my face and said, "you have fire in your eyes!"

I knew nothing of the fire, I was just flabbergasted.

I just stared wide eyed at David. David stepped back shaking, and I opened the door indicating that I wanted him to leave.

David literally ran, saying as he went, "don't look at me with fire in your eyes!"

All I can say is God must have put what David described as, "fire in my eyes." I believe God frightened him away because I didn't have the strength to stand against what was happening. I should have known better.....

Middle Eastern men especially those from arab countries are very determined and forceful, much more so than from other countries.

David phoned and lamely apologized. I told him I didn't know what got into him.

"I love you," he said.

I reminded him that I'm almost old enough to be his mother. Fifteen years difference in age didn't bother him in the least. It sure bothered me, and besides he isn't a believer. What in the world was I going to do with him?

The more I told him I wasn't interested in anything other than a friendship, the more he pursued me. He didn't want to hear about Jesus, but he wanted to be a part of my life.

"I love your mentality," he kept telling me.

Months went by and his sweet Israeli talk was having a weakening effect on me. The Lord showed me that I was on dangerous ground. The truth was that I was a little in love too, and when you are a little in love you do silly things.

David represented temptation to me. In my saner moments I knew David had the capability of destroying me, by destroying my witness. "How could an Ambassador for Jesus Christ be feeling this way," I marveled. "Surely the Lord would protect me," I reasoned.

Yet again, we agreed to meet for coffee at our original place. As I was walking to our prearranged meeting place, something awful happened. Awful I say, but maybe it wasn't so awful. Sometimes it's better to take our punishment in this life, rather than the next.....

I knew I shouldn't be meeting him, but in disobedience I went anyway. I was tripping down the road in my high heel shoes and the next thing I knew I was flung into the air. I lost my footing and came crashing down full force on my face on the dirty pavement.

How I didn't break my cheekbone was a wonder. The full force of my body hitting the ground could have resulted in more serious problems.

By the time I stood up I was dazed and blood was all over my face. Within minutes my face showed severe bruising and swelling and I wasn't a pretty picture.

Crying, I protected my face with my hand, turned around in my tracks and came home.

I called David and told him what had just happened. He was shocked, but his response was, "you just fell, Maureen. It had nothing to do with coming to meet me."

I knew better, it had everything to do with meeting David. David is dangerously unsaved and has no desire to come to the Lord. All he was doing was drawing me away from God. In my foolishness I had silenced the voice of truth that warned me to keep away from David. Drastic measures were put in place to stop me. Now I understand that indeed God is a jealous God and what's more, I'm pleased with the chastisement, for those God loves, He chastises.

My face has healed and my lesson learned. Praise God I'm restored to right relationship with my Father and hopefully no beautiful big brown eyes will tempt me again.

I'm also not going to stop smiling. I just trust God will keep me safe in the palm of His hand, wherein there is joy everlasting..

PART II

~ LOVE, A DIFFERENT PERSPECTIVE ~

Chapter 11

Come To Jerusalem

Written by: Bill Williamson

"When are you coming to Jerusalem?" Maureen asked.

"I'd like to, but I cannot go running around the world unless it's the Lord's will," I said into the receiver of the phone.

"It is the Lord's will that you come," she replied with such confidence.

For the past dozen years I had been on a course following the Lord explicitly, and I wanted nothing of the things of the world. My days of chasing after my own pleasure, and seeking my own best, were over. Now my every effort was to see God glorified through everything in my life. I couldn't fly off to Israel, or anywhere else for that matter, merely because I thought it was a good idea. But, I could not put the thought out of my mind. "Come to Jerusalem," the idea intrigued me.

I have become accustomed to 'quiet times' every morning as part of my life. This is my way of focusing daily upon God, and setting my heart towards Him for the day. I pray, listen, and read His Word, the Bible. It is a joyous time. It hasn't always been that way, but through determination and persistence over the years, it has become a lifestyle. I now depend upon the Lord's input in all phases of my life.

The day following my phone conversation with Maureen, I settled into my 'quiet time,' and my thoughts turned to Israel. After a time of prayer about her request to come, I asked my Lord, "What do you say, Lord?" Three times in my daily Bible reading that morning I found reference to, "Coming to Jerusalem."

I continued in prayer for a few days, and soon knew in my spirit, Israel was part of what God had for my life. I began to plan my trip to Jerusalem.

By now you're probably asking, "What was your connection to Maureen? Why were you talking to her by telephone anyway?" Let me explain.

Seventeen years earlier Maureen had traveled from Israel to Hawaii to take part in a Discipleship Training School, (DTS), with Youth With A Mission, (YWAM). While in the school, Maureen made a good friend named, Judith. One year later, Judith took a staff position in a new YWAM work in Montana. She had been there just over a year when I joined the Montana DTS as a student.

I met Judith, and after becoming better acquainted, and finding God's leading, we decided to marry. Judith and I did marry after the completion of my DTS.

Because writing was a love of mine, and not one of Judith's, I began corresponding with all of Judith's friends on her behalf. Maureen was one of the faithful ones who had kept writing to Judith and her two sons after their time in Hawaii.

Judith died of lung cancer after we had been married ten wonderful years. I continued writing to Maureen as I went on with the lifestyle Judith and I had established, that is seeking after God and serving Him any way that He asked. We had developed an attitude of, "Yes, Lord," to anything He asked of us.

For a while after Judith's death, I helped friends with short term church outreaches into Mexico, until I knew the Lord was leading me to work with YWAM in Colorado. While in Colorado I led a DTS team of young people to India. For two months the eight students and I endured great hardship, as our money, passports, and airline tickets were stolen early in the outreach. I had prayed for a radical outreach for these young people, and God delivered. It was a time of seeing God's faithfulness to us that would never be forgotten by any of us.

I left YWAM Colorado behind and was serving with a Pastor friend in a new church plant in Boulder City, Nevada. God had spoken specifically to me about coming and giving six months in administrative helps. My agreement of six months would come to completion on August 6th.

May arrived, and I was absolutely sure that I was to travel to Israel. I thought at that time it was part of a trip that included: Kenya, Israel, and then the Czech Republic to work with YWAM. Before May was out, both Kenya, and Czech Republic dropped from my travel plans. Only Israel was left. I ordered my tickets.

I came to Boulder City with very little. I had acquired an apartment and a splattering of second hand furniture, that included cardboard boxes for end tables. My living room served as my office, with a make shift desk for my computer items. Most of my time was spent remodeling an old dress shop for our new storefront church, and organizing a church office. I spent my limited free time editing and preparing Maureen's latest manuscript. Her previous publisher in South Africa had gone bankrupt and returned her manuscript. Subsequently, Maureen asked if I could possibly help search for publishers in the USA. I promptly agreed.

Maureen and I began talking more by phone because of the manuscript. The middle of August rolled around and we both had great anticipation of finally meeting. It had been fifteen years of writing from half way around the world.

My flight took me from Las Vegas to Atlanta, on to Switzerland for a short layover, and then the final leg to Israel. My final seat assignment to Tel Aviv left a lot to be desired. I sat in the plane's middle section, seemingly miles from any window. I strained to see what lie below as we approached Israel. I was allowed no preview. But soon my feet hit Israeli soil, and I followed the crowd through the terminal, searching for anything written in English. Why should I be surprised that everything was in Hebrew, but I was. I found the line appropriate for me and quickly passed through showing only my passport.

Maureen and I had agreed that I would make my own way from Tel Aviv to Tchernikovsky Street in Jerusalem, where she operated a successful Bed and Breakfast. I stepped outside the terminal at Ben Gurion International Airport into the bright Israeli sunshine, and after a bit of confusion over the availability of a Sherot, (a van used for taxi), I opted for a regular taxi. The driver offered the same fare to share a ride with three others going to Jerusalem, but no wait was required.

I found out how green I was after arrival in Jerusalem when the other three passengers, all Jewish, were delivered and I found myself alone with the taxi driver. He demanded fifty shekels after quoting me thirty-four in Tel Aviv. He was unwilling to use English, and I felt forced to contribute sixteen shekels towards my new 'experience' in Israel.

A bit sweaty, frustrated by the dishonest taxi driver, but glad to have arrived, I peered beyond the tall, white, metal fence that separated Maureen's apartment from the street. Her apartment was slightly elevated from the street level. Her rather large dining room window could be seen through the greenery of a beautiful Syringa tree. The large slider window was open and there was Maureen, nicely attired in blue, green, and white, waving to me. A beautiful picture. She disappeared from the window, and the taxi pulled away as I moved my bags beyond the white fence.

Maureen reappeared at the building entrance and moved to meet me on the sidewalk. We stood, embraced briefly, and looked at each other face to face for the first time ever.

There was a little nervousness as we moved inside her apartment. Maureen had prepared a beautiful plate of nuts, grapes, and other delicious fruit for my arrival. We talked, enjoyed a walk around the neighborhood, and soon it was early evening. Maureen called another taxi that carried me to a Bed and Breakfast in Meveseret Zion, some fifteen miles west of Jerusalem. Maureen had a strict rule in her B&B, 'no men stayed there, unless part of a married couple.' She didn't want even the appearance of evil in her home. The next day I would return, and the adventure would begin.

My first morning in Israel came, and I boarded a bus that took me into the heart of the Lord's city, Jerusalem. It was busy, noisy, and totally foreign to me. Israeli soldiers in their OD Green uniforms, most with automatic weapons, were everywhere.

Hasidic Jews, dressed in their black garb, moved hastily along the streets. As the bus pulled into the bus stop, I spotted Maureen waiting at the curbside.

I learned quickly that walking was a way of life for Maureen in the Holy City. She traveled incredible distances in her fashionable high heel shoes. Maureen considers herself an Ambassador, an Ambassador for Christ, and she dresses and always looks the part. This, my first full day in Jerusalem, was no exception. We visited the Shuk, an open market with isles and rows of vegetables, fruits, and all kinds of other sundries. I found the smells that wafted along the narrow passageways were strange to my senses, and merchants were yelling much too loudly promoting their goods.

We followed the smell of fresh baked bread into a bakery and purchased Zata Bread. Zata is a dark green spice mix that is often spread over the top of a large round, flat bread. Bread thicker than pizza crust, and delightfully delicious, as is all Israeli bread. We found a nearby wall, so typical of Jerusalem, and sat upon it eating our Zata Bread. The city's busyness passed us by and we seemed oblivious to it all, as our smiles and teeth became coated and framed by green Zata.

We visited Ben Yehuda Street, which is a pedestrian mall where International tourist congregate to buy coffees, cold drinks, Falafels, (Pita Breads stuffed with vegetables and falafel balls made of Chick Pea), wonderful Israeli ice cream, and many other delights. Intermingled in the crowds were many local performers attempting to get a shekel or two from the passing tourists playing instruments, operating puppets, and even group singing.

There were others who simply held out a hand to us. One such bearded character was pirate like in his dirty appearance, wearing black hat, clothing, and cloak. He was actually fitted with a wooden peg leg, and hobbled along on a rough made crutch. His appearance seemed to scare people away, rather than entice them to give.

One elderly man who held a violin across his lap, sat slumped in his small wooden chair with his eyes closed, and appeared to be napping. His dark hat, and gray suit, were unkept and dirty. His feet were clad with worn house slippers, and I imagined they would produce holes in the soles if visible. He hadn't shaved in days.

The idea was that he would play the violin, people would have compassion, and in a move of charity, give him some amount of money. However, this man was obviously very tired of the whole routine. Maureen, speaking in Hebrew, asked him to play a well known Israeli tune. He responded with a great deal of frustration, a wave of his hand, and said, "Can't you just give me the money?" Maureen gave him a kiss, and the money. He was another of Maureen's many street friends. He smiled and looked pleased as we moved on.

Then there was Abraham, without legs and confined to a wheel chair. His wheel chair was draped with plastic bags containing a half eaten sandwich, a dry bread roll, and other odds and ends found along Ben Yehuda Street. As we approached, Abraham's smile broadened, exposing gaping holes where teeth had been at one time. He was fond of Maureen, as she always had smile, a touch, and a greeting for him. Maureen grasped his dirty hand, squeezed it, and held on to him. They chatted in a combination of Hebrew and English. He welcomed prayer.

There were more encounters with down-and-outer's that day, all happy to see Maureen. She was quite popular with the street people. She was not afraid of their smell, nor their unkept bodies. She had authentic love for them, and they for her. I was seeing something of Maureen I had not been privilege to see in the fifteen years of knowing her from afar.

My first day in Jerusalem was wonderful. The following days would be the same, and Maureen and I became inseparable.

Each day I would rise, have a light breakfast, and hike to one of the two bus stops close to me. I would arrive at Maureen's doorstep ready for more of Jerusalem, and the ongoing adventure. We began to see that we were two of a kind, in Jesus.

To be in Jerusalem and see places that I had read about in the Bible for so many years was thrilling. There was such a freedom to walk, explore and experience them all. I found Jerusalem to be a place where fear did not exist for me. I am not prone to fear in the first place, but here an extraordinary peace filled me as I moved about the city.

One night I was catching the last bus to Meveseret Zion. It was near midnight. I approached the bus stop to find one lone man, also waiting. As I entered the bus stop shelter, he looked my way and began pacing. His pacing was deliberate, and his route carried him to within inches of my face before he would turn and walk away, then back to press into my face again. All, in an attempt to intimidate me. He was like a cat, back and forth, back and forth. There was something evil within him, but I had a strange peace within me, and was not disturbed by his bizarre behavior.

The man was no more than thirty, dark skinned, and very dark hair. His eyes were also dark, and they stayed focused upon me except when he turned to pace away from me.

I calmly leaned against the wall of the shelter and watched. Each time he turned back to me, his eyes met mine. Without expression on his face, he was totally somber. I began to tire of this demonstration of his disapproval of me, and I breathed a prayer that went like this, "Lord, let the spirit in him, see the Spirit in me." I was surprised at the words of the prayer. I hadn't planned them.

At that very moment the man turned into the bus stop shelter and sat down. He did not look at me again. My peace continued, but I was amazed at what had just happened. The spirit in him had indeed seen the living Holy Spirit in me, and the standoff was settled. I was not to be intimidated by his wimpy spirit, because I had a greater Spirit within me.

This incident would be one I would long remember, even if it had happened only this once. But just a few weeks later, at another bus stop far across town, it happened again. It was the midnight hour, and the circumstances were similar. I approached the bus stop with a lone man waiting. He paced, I leaned, he stared, I prayed the same prayer, and he sat down. Same scenario, same result. Thank you, Lord for that power that lies within us, that we need not fear at all. I know too, that this is not only a peace available in Jerusalem, but wherever we tread our feet upon this earth.

For weeks Maureen and I had stayed close to Jerusalem. On this day we decided to travel by bus to the well known Massada near the Dead Sea. Massada is a mountain top site where a community of Jewish Zealots took their own lives hundreds of years ago rather than give in to demands of the Roman soldiers camped in siege at the base of the mountain. We went to Jerusalem's Main Bus Terminal by bus, and I strode to the ticket window in all my newly acquired Israeli knowledge and purchased our tickets.

After a short wait, we were on our first over the highway adventure. Maureen pointed out many interesting things along the way. Such as the hills David would have moved through with his band of rebels, as they maneuvered out of Saul's reach, and the caves that they likely hid in, as well. Along the Dead Sea, that in fact did look 'dead' because of the lack of vegetation anywhere near it, and the salt saturated soils along the shores, we saw wild Ibex, a goat with long curved horns, foraging for rare sprigs of dry grass and shrubbery amongst the rocky hillsides.

With the Dead Sea behind us, and no city or village within miles, we arrived at a lonely bus stop near the base of Massada. It was a short walk to a cluster of buildings that included a Hostel, Gift shops, restaurant, and shaded table area. Soon we were making the short walk to the aerial tramway that would take us to the top of Massada. The ride to the top itself was breathtaking.

On top, we found excavated remains of structures that had been used for housing, community center, and other parts of this mountain top community. The most interesting was the bathhouse that had been carved out of the mountain itself. The entrance was below the surface of the mountain top, and once inside, newly constructed plank walkways led us through the massive structure. Remains of the beautiful wall tiles could still be seen as they had been excavated, cleaned and rejuvenated.

We tramped over the entire top of the mountain, which was large enough to accommodate several football fields. All the while, Maureen was very elegant in her dress that displayed Zebras, Cheetahs, and flora typical of Africa. Upon her feet were her ever present high heel shoes. I was impressed at her tenacity in this area, especially when I learned that she had a metal screw that ran nearly through her right ankle as the result of a serious accident years earlier.

Finally, sun drenched, hot and sweaty, we followed the winding, narrow trail back to the Tramway for the return to the base of the mountain. Once at the bottom, and a short look around the shops, we walked the quarter mile to the bus stop. We were looking forward to our air-conditioned ride back to Jerusalem. Israeli buses are clean, comfortable, and quite modern. After a short time of huddling in the sparse shade of the tiny shelter, our bus arrived. I pulled the bus stubs from my wallet, and we stepped up into the refreshing coolness of the bus. I handed the ticket stubs to the driver.

I felt smug that I had purchased the tickets for this journey, we had made the advance on Massada, and now we would rest together on this nice bus, talking over our day as we rode back to Jerusalem.

But, my rather smug feeling left me as the driver looked from the ticket stub to me, as if to say, "What's up, buddy?" I looked intently at him as he spoke in Hebrew. I wasn't getting any of what he was saying, but there was clearly a problem. As is so typical in Israel, the passengers closest to the front of the bus began trying to help us understand. Maureen was able to put bits and pieces together, and understanding swooped down on us like a horrendous vulture. The understanding was totally for us to gain, and there was to be none by the driver. We learned that I had handed him the spent stub of a 'one-way' bus ticket. Unknown to me, I had purchased for us, one-way tickets to the desert of the Dead Sea. There was to be no return with this ticket.

Passengers were staring at us, some talking rapidly, and I suppose, wondering who this idiot of a tourist was that had brought a lady, one-way, into the desert. Although you can purchase tickets from the bus driver, I had only thirty-six shekels. Maureen had none. We tried to communicate to the driver, that I had access to money through my Bank Card once we were back in Jerusalem. He would have none of that. We either had the seventy-one shekels, or off the bus.

We stepped off the bus into the afternoon heat and onto the dusty roadside. We watched as our air-conditioned bus pulled away and disappeared in the distance. Maureen and I had laughed many times in the several weeks leading up to this Massada adventure, but laughter wasn't coming so easy now. I felt horrible at what I had done. Maureen was incredibly pleasant, and understanding. We made our way into the shade of a few trees nearby. We grasped hands and offered a prayer to our Lord, our everything, for His help.

We talked about our situation and began to smile, even laugh, over the hilarity of our circumstances. I was probably the first to buy one way tickets to Massada. That ticket clerk in Jerusalem must still be laughing.

Suddenly, I remembered a young lady had been sitting in an office of one of the gift shops near the Tramway. The thought occurred to me that she may be able to help us. We made the hot walk back to the gift shop and searched for that office, and the lady. There she was, doing paper work. I moved to her doorway and she looked up. She spoke enough English to understand our dilemma, and though she wasn't supposed to give cash advances on a Bank Card, she did advance us 100 shekels. We were delighted and quickly returned to the bus stand so as not to miss the next bus. Our first road trip together would not soon be forgotten.

The next day, with an opportunity to see Bethlehem, and meet an Arab Pastor, we set off by Arab taxi to the Israeli checkpoint located at the outskirts of Bethlehem. Several of Maureen's friends joined us, one of which shared about Jesus to the Arab driver the whole way. Coming and going into the Israeli 'Occupied Territory' of Bethlehem was not easy for Arabs. Specific papers are required. Israel is in control. But Bethlehem is Arab, Moslem in faith, and about 30,000 in population. Pastor Issa said there are only about thirty born again believers who live there.

Pastor Issa met us at the checkpoint, and I had already climbed into the dusty back seat of his car, when an Arab ran up to the car yelling. He was our previous taxi driver and he had my day pack in his hand. The bag carried my camera, passport, money, everything important I had brought with me to Bethlehem. I had left it laying in the back seat of his taxi. After traveling some distance back toward Jerusalem he had discovered it, and was intent on returning it to me. I was impressed with this man's integrity.

We continued on into Bethlehem in Pastor Issa's car. The car defies description. The shocks had either been removed, or they had forgotten their purpose. We bounced along streets that were a combination of stone, dirt, asphalt, and concrete. It seemed that everything in Bethlehem was under construction. Trenches, piles of dirt, detours, and dust, was the commonplace.

We wound through the narrow, windy streets as if lost. Many streets were blocked by the ongoing construction, or was it, destruction? Pastor Issa detoured to Boaz's Field, stopped the car, and all five of us piled out. No one had said anything about stopping or seeing this Biblically historic site, but I was delighted. I had always enjoyed the Book of Ruth where the story of Boaz and Ruth unfolds. The sun was blazing and the heat was intense. The little road that ran by the field was deep in a fine dust that drifted everywhere as the car rolled to a stop.

Maureen and I found ourselves posing alongside a short stone wall topped with cyclone fencing that separated the road from the field. A beer bottle lay in the dust near our feet and other trash was strewn along the roadside, common place in Arab villages. The field was now planted with Olive trees rather than grain as in the days of Boaz and Ruth. As the photo was being taken, I wondered, would Maureen and I be like Ruth and Boaz.

We were soon stopped again in front of a building on an extremely narrow street that could more easily be described as an alleyway. The building contained Pastor Issa's church and home, the church below and the home above. We met his children and his wife, Diana. They fed us a fine Arab lunch before we gathered in their living room for a time of prayer. It was during this time that Pastor Issa had words for many of us. For Maureen and I, he spoke words that related to changes coming, and doors that would be opened to us. God had something in mind for us.....

For one month Maureen and I had not parted company, except when I would leave for my own quarters in the evening. We had become fast friends and our relationship had been absolutely Godly in every way. This friendship was built upon a foundation of knowing each other's Godly character, and this 'knowing' had come from watching the other's life from afar for fifteen years. We had always admired what we saw in regard to the willingness to forsake everything and follow Jesus Christ. Being together non-stop for thirty days had only confirmed what we already knew.

About a year before coming to Israel I had felt a longing to be married once again. I missed Judith, whom I lost to Lung Cancer. I remember saying, "Lord, if you bring me another wife, I would like her to be someone like, Maureen." Not because I had designs on Maureen, but because I so admired her character. A character built upon Father God Himself. I hadn't thought that I our lives would ever intermingle because we dwelt on opposite sides of the earth.

Still continuing my early morning 'quiet times' with the Lord while in Israel, I began seeking Father God about what role Maureen was to play in my life. It wasn't long before I knew in my heart that she was the one I wanted to spend the rest of my life with. I felt I had God's approval to ask her to marry me, and I asked the Lord to let me know when it was time. That time came much sooner than I expected. I felt it was right, and I asked, "How shall I ask her, Lord?"

His answer shocked me. I was to share four things with her. I include them directly from my journal:

1. My view of my life of service to Jesus...

2. Reading of Ephesians 4:29 - 5:23 (A husband's responsibility to a wife.)

3. Wash her feet, (Maureen's), in a display of servanthood to her.

4. Pop the question!

Thank you, Father.

I asked, 'when,' and I felt that was up to me.

Today seems right.

What a great start for a wonderful day. I was to ask Maureen to marry me! But, the rest of the day didn't follow suit. Maureen received a disturbing call from a dear saint and friend, and was visibly upset.

Maureen enjoyed retiring with a bath around 7:00 PM, and that time was approaching. I thought, "The timing just isn't right." It was at this moment I saw a tiny tear form in the corner of Maureen's eye. I moved to her and simply held her. And at that moment, somehow, the timing did seem right. Circumstances don't always dictate what we should, or should not do. This time it was the opposite of what I had thought only moments earlier.

I told Maureen that I had some things to share with her and asked if we could take the time. She smiled, nodded her head, and whispered, "Yes." We moved to the wicker 'love seat' that made up part of her living room furnishings. I slowly went through the four items listed in my journal.

I spoke of my devotion to Jesus, and my plan to follow Him wherever he may lead. I shared that I had not been called to a specific length of time in Israel, and didn't know when the Lord may ask me to move on.

I read Paul's instructions to husbands from Ephesians and explained how important they were to me. I excluded verses 22-24 where Paul talked about wives responsibilities.

I asked her to bring me a basin and a towel. I washed her feet.

Still on my knees after washing her feet, I took her hand and looked up into her eyes. There was evidence of tears as I told her I wanted her to become my wife, if she wanted to share in my life of service to Jesus as described. I told her it was my desire to share the rest of my life with her. I asked that she answer only when she was ready...there was no rush.

Maureen did not answer specifically. We enjoyed much peace together as we embraced, and sat together talking, laughing, and just being close. We reluctantly parted around 10:00 PM, extremely late for the two of us to be together.

I enjoyed the cool night air strolling back to my new lodging twenty minutes away, munching glazed almonds Maureen had given me for the walk home. I wrote the following in my journal that night:

"Thank you, Lord for your goodness, and your gift to me of, Maureen. Be with us always."

Now, if she would only say yes!"

Chapter 12

Friendly Takeover

Written by: Bill Williamson

"Friendly Takeover?"   You're thinking, "What does that mean?"

Maureen and I visited a ninety-two year old friend recently. He was talking about his stocks, and how in the corporate world companies take one another over, sometimes in a hostile way, and sometimes, friendly.   Sy said, "It's like the two of you," and he looked at Maureen, "you take over him," he pointed at me, "and if he doesn't resist, it's a 'Friendly Takeover.'"   He smiled.

When two companies decide on a 'Friendly Takeover,' they merge into one.   Each company is strong, but together they are stronger.   Their future becomes more productive, and more profit comes from it. They enjoy a mutual benefit. In a hostile takeover, the opposite is true. A strong company forces itself upon a weaker one, and there is little benefit, and often the result is loss, or failure for both.

A marriage can be a 'Friendly Takeover,' where two strong individuals come together and they are stronger, they are one, they agree, and are more productive. One does not dominate, but both are important and involved in the merger. There is much joy and contentment, happiness results.

Some marriages are like the hostile takeover, one dominates to the detriment of the other. There is little joy, and they often fail.

Scripture speaks about man and wife in Mark 10:8-9, "...and the two shall become one flesh; consequently they are no longer two, but one flesh." NAS. The 'Friendly Takeover' was God's plan from the beginning.

This chapter is about a 'Friendly Takeover.' The merger of Bill Williamson, and Maureen Woods.

~~~~~~~

Jaffa Street was busy as usual. We ducked into a jewelry store to look at rings. This had become a regular occurrence since Maureen had finally said, "Yes!" A full month after I had popped the question she consented to marrying me.

A look at the jewelry cases revealed the one ring we were looking for was not available. We stepped back onto Jaffa street into a great commotion. Traffic was stopped, pedestrian's were restrained on the sidewalks, and Israeli police were everywhere. The greatest intensity of the problem was back half a block, near the Shuk, (market place), where we had just come from. The familiar Israeli bomb squads were in action. Someone had left unattended parcels in the Shuk. People were rushed out, and the area cleared, so that police could examine and detonate if necessary.

This was common place in Israel. In the short time I had been in Jerusalem, I had encountered this situation in the Main Post Office, Bus Station, and now the Shuk.

Soon the parcel was declared safe, and the traffic that had backed up miles, was now free to begin movement. We too, were walking back toward city center.

"But wait," you're probably saying, "how did the 'yes' happen?"

Maureen and I confided with close friends, who lived in the center of Jerusalem, of my proposal, and her contemplative answer. They prayed with us, and provided a very wise suggestion. "Why not withdraw away from one another for a short period, maybe three days, and seek the Lord? Let Him show you if it's right or wrong," they said.

We did just that. I went to the Galilee for three days and stayed in Tiberias at the Scottish Inn. I had a quaint little stone cottage in back of the main hotel, Number 17. It was a perfect place for me to have three quiet, prayerful days. Maureen stayed in her apartment with the same intent, to pray and seek Father's advice.

Once settled into Number 17, I walked along the shores of the Sea of Galilee. I was in awe as I thought of all that had taken place on these shores. Jesus had called many of His Disciples here, maybe right where I strolled. Surely some of them had prayed through serious matters here in Tiberias too.

Once back in my room, I read the daily reading from my devotional by Charles Spurgeon. I was blessed at the scripture found there. It said, *"He goeth before you into Galilee; There shall ye see Him, as he said unto you."* Mark 16:7.

God is so faithful to let us know that we are on track. He delights in surprising us with little gifts. No, big gifts! Why was I here, at the Galilee this particular day? Only God knows for sure, but I so appreciate His loving kindness to me to let me know He's with me.

My stay at the Galilee was to be a test, as I was struck with fever and unable to do much but lay on my bed. I rose on several occasions over the three days and walked to the Sea of Galilee, or to the center of Tiberias. Although sick with fever, I knew God was with me, and that he was doing a work for Maureen and I. I called Maureen the second day and asked her to pray for me. That night the fever left me. My last day I was weak and barely able to carry my bag the five blocks to the bus station.

In Jerusalem, Maureen stated she had not received a specific word about us from the Lord, but earlier she had felt led of the Lord to, honor me, stand with me, and decrease while I increase. I wrote in my journal on that day, "Who am I, Lord, to deserve this?" Surely it's true what several people spoke to me before leaving America, "You shall be blessed in Israel."

In a few short days, the news came. There were no whistles, bells, horns, or any other extraordinary evidence, but Maureen finally, 'knew that she knew.' She was to say, "Yes!"

We asked an Arab friend in Bethlehem, Pastor Issa, to marry us. We knew no one else in Bethlehem, and the ceremony could be kept simple. A problem developed, Pastor Issa was not licensed to do marriages in Israel. He quickly recommended Dr. Khoury, Pastor of the First Baptist Church of Bethlehem. We spoke with him and soon the plans were set. Pastor Issa would stand with me as best man.

Then there was the Israeli woman simply known as 'Miri.' She made it known as soon as she heard of our wedding plans, that she wouldn't have it any other way, she would be Maureen's 'Flower Girl.'

The date was set for November 10th. Everything was a go. There would be no guests, only Maureen and I, with Pastor Issa and

Miri. And of course, Dr. Khoury. We had not intended to elope, but it did look that way.

On the Sunday prior to the wedding, I was in my apartment in Ma Alé Adumin preparing for a morning church service. I coughed as I bent over the basin brushing my teeth. There was a familiar sting in my lower back, and I knew I had damaged a muscle. But, only in a minor way, I hoped. I went on to church. I had much difficulty sitting through the service because of the increasing pain. Afterwards we were given a ride to Maureen's apartment.

In pain, I lay down on her bed for some relief. After several hours, it was obvious I couldn't rise from the bed. I finally slipped to the floor on my knees, and with help, could stand and shuffle my feet along the smooth tile floor. I was assisted to one of Maureen's Bed and Breakfast guest rooms, and onto a single bed.

It was clear that the wedding would not take place on the 10th. We called Dr. Khoury and postponed two days.

For two more days I lay flat on my back, unable to move. I had torn a muscle in my lower back. I called it a 'familiar pain' earlier because I had torn muscles in that same area before. Pastor Issa came from Bethlehem and prayed for my recovery. He advised me to continue trying to move.

On the third day of my agony, I purposed to move, as Pastor Issa had counseled. I was able to roll to my right, with great pain. I then thought, "Maybe I can sit on the side of the bed." Success, I was able to do it! Then I stood, shuffled my feet along, and I made my way into the living area lounge. By the next day I had improved, and was able to accompany Maureen into Jerusalem by bus, and pick up my borrowed wedding clothes.

Wedding day arrived, November 12th, and a taxi was called. We picked up Miri on Asa street and went directly to the Israeli checkpoint outside Bethlehem. Pastor Issa met us with his familiar, and dusty, car. He took us to the church, which stood two stories high on a steep hillside overlooking Shepard's Field. Arab graffiti had been spray painted on the courtyard walls around the church. The five foot high concrete wall had wire fencing and barbed wire mounted on it to a height of about nine feet. It looked like a stockade.

The ceremony took place in the sanctuary, and was no more than ten minutes in length. Pastor Khoury's oldest son snapped our only wedding pictures with our inexpensive automatic camera.

We were in the Pastor's office taking care of paperwork after the ceremony, and Miri exclaimed to me, "You didn't give her the ring!" Somehow the ring portion of the ceremony had been omitted. Under Yasser Arafat's watchful eye from a picture on the wall, we presented rings to one another, taking another minute and a half. A wedding ceremony far from the usual, but a cherished memory of ours to this day.

Pastor Issa dropped us back at the checkpoint where heavy traffic was waiting for clearance out of Bethlehem. A crude concrete and wire shelter provided cover for the Israeli soldiers manning the checkpoint. There were many soldiers, and weapons. Arabs were required to have papers of permission to leave 'Occupied Territory.' It was more difficult getting out of Bethlehem, than in.

Miri, Maureen and I stood looking for a taxi to take us back to Jerusalem. We had been at this checkpoint before, but this time Maureen and I were one, Mr. and Mrs. Williamson.

As we waited, one nice car in the line pulled alongside us. Miri looked at the driver, and stuck her thumb out. The man signaled us to get in. We looked at one another, shrugged our shoulders, and jumped in. He was a very obliging and pleasant businessman from Scotland. He dropped us on Jaffa Street near the Old

City and sped away. Miri continued down the street in her bright yellow dress, carrying her bouquet. We made our way to our favorite café for a celebration lunch, before catching a taxi to Maureen's home on Tchernikovsky Street that would now become our's.

We spent the next two days resting and just getting to know each other around home. Sunday arrived and our Sherut, (taxi van), arrived to take us to the airport. I was still unable to lift or carry anything of significant weight. Maureen carried our bags, while I carried her purse. What a sight we must have been. We were off on a four day honeymoon to Turkey. (A trip out of Israel was also required by both of us for Visa renewal, as our three month Tourist Visa's were about to expire.)

On the plane, we found our seats, and only then realized the ticket agent had done exactly what we had requested. We had been assigned isle seats. Now that doesn't sound so alarming, but when you think about it, how can both of us have isle seats? Only one way! We were seated across the isle from one another. On honeymoon, and not seated together. Once again we laughed. We got used to the idea and Maureen was soon talking to an Arab couple next to her about Jesus. We passed notes across the isle, and occasionally held hands, the kind of things newlyweds do. We were thankful the flight was less than two hours.

Money was not an issue with us, because we had so little of it. After the bit of wedding expense we had incurred, we had only fifty US dollars. But that would be sufficient for our honeymoon, as our Turkey package already had been paid, and it included air fare, hotel, and breakfast and dinner buffet daily.

On the ground in Turkey, we proceeded through the airport. At Immigration, I was informed, as an American, I needed a Visa. After being guided to the proper place, I presented my passport. "Forty-five dollars," the Officer stated. I placed my fifty dollars before him and he passed five back to me. We now had only five dollars for our honeymoon. Laughter again was the order of the day as we left the airport into the dark and rainy Turkish night. We climbed into the waiting shuttle bus, Maureen still carrying the luggage, and I carrying her purse.

Hotel Club Sara was Five Star, with magnificent tile floors, beautiful chandeliers, and an array of well coordinated wall hangings The desk clerk was hospitable, and once he heard that we were on honeymoon, an upgrade of our accommodations was made. We were moved to a garden bungalow. And garden it was, the vegetation was lush, deep, and beautiful.

Our upgraded quarters were delightful. There was nicely done wood throughout, indirect lighting, and ample conveniences. One shortcoming was noticed, but that was not until we made ready for bed. We had arrived in a steady downpour of rain. This would not have bothered us, but the rainwater from the roof of our bungalow had found a way through the roof, ceiling, and onto our bed. One half of the bed was quite soaked.

Half a bed was all that was required, however. We had a delightful rest, and the next morning we informed the hotel staff of our leak dilemma. The staff was very apologetic and quickly upgraded us again. We were moved within the same garden area to another bungalow. This one was even nicer, with much more room, and finer in every way. And, there were no leaks.

Five dollars spending money meant that we would carefully consider where each dollar went. Our first full day in Antalya had a scheduled free bus tour. 'Free' was to our liking and we joyfully went along. We gave one dollar to the bus driver as a tip, as did all the other passengers.

Our second day, we hopped on a local bus and found our way to the center of the ancient city of Antalya. Even though my back was still causing me pain, and kept me from really stepping out, we enjoyed walking through some of the 'Old City' and the new. My mind was so much on my back pain, that at one point I laid our camera down on a park bench, where we sat overlooking the ancient sea harbor, and forgot to pick it up as we walked on. We lost some of our wedding pictures, and all that we had taken in Antalya for a day and a half.

Our four days in Antalya passed quickly. Our five American dollars had gone for two tips, two photographs of Maureen and I, and one bus fare into the city. Soon we were back in Jerusalem to begin daily life as Christian man and wife.

We were to be tested immediately.

It was Vivian on the phone. Vivian was our marvelous Israeli landlady. "Can I come and get the rent today?" was her question. Vivian preferred coming personally for the rent. This suited us because there was opportunity to share our life of faith in Jesus every month.

I paused, knowing in my mind that we did not have the full rent amount. "Sure, that'll be fine," I said.

"I'll be there about 2:00 P.M.," she responded.

The rent was seven hundred, U.S. dollars. We not only did-n't have it all, we saw no way that we could get it. But Vivian was coming at 2:00 P.M. Maureen and I prayed, knowing that God would make a way. He had been faithful both to Maureen and I independently before our marriage, why would He change now that we were married? He would not. He would certainly meet our every need, or make a way.

Two o'clock came, the phone rang. "I can't come today, how about tomorrow?" Vivian said.

"No problem, tomorrow will be fine," I stated. But under my breath I was saying, "Praise you, Lord!" He had made a way, where there seemed to be no way.

Tomorrow arrived, and so did the money, from an unexpected source. When Vivian arrived, we joyfully placed the rent money on the table before her. This was just another in a long string of months that Maureen had been able to pay miraculously. Vivian had leased the apartment to Maureen even when she had said, "I have no money, no job, but God will provide." It was a miracle that Vivian had trusted Maureen. Maureen trusted God, and because she did, He never failed her.

Maureen and I wanted people to know that they could trust us. Once we were trusted, there was a better chance they would believe what we shared with them about Jesus. Besides that, God desires us to be a people with integrity, people with no compromise. On two occasions, Miki, our money changer on Ben Yehuda, had short changed himself when he had exchanged our personal checks for shekels. Miki is a very sharp man, he is not prone to making mistakes, but both times Miki shorted himself more than 800 shekels. That's $200. Not small mistakes.

Each time, I was out of his shop and up the street before I discovered the mistake. I joyfully returned the overpayment, to his amazement. I noticed after that, Miki would round up the amount in my favor. A mutual appreciation of respect prevailed.

Our's was a happy home. Praise and worship music played continuously in the apartment and was filled with peace and much laughter. Daily we would catch bus 22 into Jerusalem, pick up mail at the main post office, and take care of any other business at hand. But, the best part was to see the people on the streets and in the shops. Many in Jerusalem knew Maureen, and delighted in her; and she in them.

One of these, was American, and had been in Israel for more than twenty years. All of these years he had taken a stand for Jesus, and was dedicated to the announcement to the Jews, that Jesus is the Messiah. He was dedicated to the point of burning his American Passport. He never intended to leave Israel. This friend was quite vocal in his criticism of Israeli policy against Christians, and spreading of the gospel.

Late one night, the Jerusalem Police swooped down on his dwelling and upended the place. Our friend was apprehended, along with seven of his friends. They were held at Ramla Prison on charges of Visa violation. Maureen received a call from Ramla, and her friend of twenty years. "Can you come? Can you bring me a few things, a King James Version Bible, and some toilet articles?"

Maureen and I began to search for a Bible. We had no money to make the purchase, but believed that one of the Christian organizations in Jerusalem would surely donate one for a brother in prison. We were wrong. We visited three such groups that had the bibles, but none would provide us one free of charge. There was much fear. We wondered, "Where's the love?"

Maureen has a wonderful American friend who has lived in Israel in the past and now visits regularly. She too was a long time friend of the man in Ramla Prison. When she heard of our plight, Norma quickly joined us. She provided the money for the Bible, and also for many other essential items. Norma drove us to Ramla in her rented car. After a hour and a half waiting in the hot sun outside the less than dignified entrance to the prison, we were allowed in. All the gifts we had brought were stripped from us, except the toothpaste. Our friend was not allowed to have even the Bible.

We were eventually escorted to a cell block where prisoners were lined against the bars that separated them from their visitors. Our friend was pointed out to us and we went to him. His appearance was excellent. He was dressed nicely and clean shaven. His countenance was great. He wore a wide smile as we approached. We grasped hands through the bars.

It was apparent he was not discouraged by the imprisonment. Our friend told us how he had prayed for many, and God was touching lives, and healing some of sickness. He had been instructed to stop praying for others, but they continued to come to his cell for prayer. The prayers continued as long they came. Like Peter and John, he was not intimidated by their orders to stop.

A few moments into our visit, he said he had something for us. He asked me to receive it through the bottom of the bars, and he slid it out. The bars began at about chest height from the top of a stub concrete wall. I glanced around at the guards as a tiny roll of paper was passed to me, and I quickly shoved it into my pocket. Our friend gave us instruction where to take it. It was rent for his apartment. The roll contained six hundred dollars. Even while in prison he was not going to forsake his financial obligation to his landlord. This was another demonstration of integrity that needs to be found in the Body of Christ, the Church.

We learned the following day by radio broadcast that our friend had been deported back to the United States, the very night we saw him.

Persecution of believers is commonplace in Israel. There are laws on the books that prevent a Christian from speaking to a youth about Jesus. Doing so can result in five years in prison. Many motions have come before the Knesset, (government), to make the same penalty for those who share Jesus with anyone. One such proposal would even make it punishable by five years in prison for carrying a New Testament publicly on the streets.

Maureen and I were taking a short cut through a well known alleyway, actually a pedestrian way, that led past a restaurant owned and operated by a sister in Christ. A great commotion was underway. Harsh words were shouted, and shoving was taking place. A group of radical young Yeshiva students were protesting the restaurant of our friend. They were accusing her of holding missionary meetings. The demonstration was for the purpose of discouraging Israeli's from patronizing her establishment. They had done previous damage to her business in this way.

In Israel, we attempt to honor the culture, the beliefs, and even the laws, as long as they do not violate what God requires of us as His servants. We must not compromise our faith though. Sadly some do, out of fear. Fear of the authorities, and fear of the masses. This sister in the Lord, was not compromising Jesus, and she often paid a price.

Maureen and I were on a side street of Ben Yehuda pedestrian mall about midday talking to a Jewish believer. Our discussion was of a serious nature, concerning help for immigrating Messianic Jews, (a Jew who believes that Jesus is the Messiah). Israel is not open to any Jew who proclaims Jesus as the Messiah, and therefore special measures are required for immigration. The content of our discussion is not really relevant here, but as we talked, a well known police informant, passed by. He stopped a short distance away, aimed his camera, and shot at least one photograph of the three of us.

Maureen and I are sure there is a Police file containing a record of our activities, even photos. Not because we broke any laws, but because we are outspoken concerning our faith. We don't hesitate to talk to someone about Jesus on the bus, on the street, or even in the Police Station, given the opportunity. We do not operate in fear. Psalms 27:1 says it best, *"The LORD is my light and my salvation; whom shall I fear? The LORD is the strength of my life; of whom shall I be afraid?"*

Another friend, Greg, and I set off to the Arab city of Ramallah just north of Jerusalem to use the rather inexpensive computers for hire. Maureen and I had composed a newsletter for our many friends around the world and needed only to reproduce it before mailing. Maureen had packed us a nice lunch with salad, boiled egg, and pita bread. After finishing our computer tasks we found a nice place in the sunshine where we could sit on a short wall and have our lunch. The wall circled an empty lot where a building had been demolished and removed. We were quite visible from the busy streets.

About half way through our lunch, both of us popping boiled egg into our mouth, it occurred to us, "This is Ramadan!" Ramadan is a thirty day time of fasting for the Moslem faith. This city, heavily Moslem, was deeply involved in Ramadan. The fast demands that they not eat at all between sunup and sundown. After that they could eat all they desire, and many did. Often it would be feast time throughout the night until sunup when the fast would start again.

Greg and I quickly put our remaining lunch out of sight, and moved on to look for a taxi home. We did this in honor of the people. We don't choose to honor the fast, or the Moslem faith, only the people. We don't believe in what they are doing, but we refuse to throw it in their faces. There is a place of respect for others, no matter what their belief is. We hope by our actions we might gain their trust, so that they will listen to what we believe the truth is.

God was building our trust in Him daily in Jerusalem. Maureen and I faced many days when provisions ran low. Sometimes I would head for the Shuk, with only about twelve shekels, ($3.00), to pick up essentials. If I was willing to shop carefully, I could fill my day pack to overflowing with fruits, vegetables, nuts, popcorn, nearly anything we needed. Dry goods were sold from large burlap bags, as it must have been in Bible days, and the unit price was low. Twelve shekels would keep us going for a few days.

At times we didn't have the twelve shekels. One Sunday night Maureen and I attended a church service at Bow Of Victory, a fellowship led by an Israeli Pastor. Bow of Victory was one of the churches we attended in Jerusalem. I say, 'one,' because we attended several. The Body of Christ enjoyed gathering in Jerusalem, we routinely attended three different churches every week, and so did many others. It came time for the offering, and we had little. I pulled what I had from my pocket, seven shekels. I felt the Lord tell me to give it all, even though I had planned a trip to the Shuk the next day, as our cupboards were bare once again. I did give it all.

The next day brought blessing from all directions, $3100 U.S. had come to us before the day finished. We need not fear giving all that we have. Luke 6:38 tells us, *"Give, and it shall be given unto you; good measure, pressed down, and shaken together, and running over, shall men give into your bosom."*

Blessings come in many forms. The festivals and holidays were a special time for us. Not only the Jewish festivals and special days, but our traditional American times as well. Christians around the world celebrate Christmas as the birth of Jesus, the Messiah. They also celebrate His resurrection from death on Easter.

Christmas Eve found us once again at the Israeli checkpoint into Bethlehem. The roads were packed with cars, buses, and people walking. They came from all over the world to gather in Manger Square of Bethlehem on Christmas Eve. Some were there for the tourist aspect of it, others because they had some degree of spirituality and this was a pilgrimage for them. But we were there for a different reason.

We were a dozen believers from several congregations in Jerusalem that had come for the specific purpose to tell others about Jesus. We wanted them to know what He had done for us, and for them. We wanted others to have the opportunity to know, and accept Him personally, as we had. We wanted them to have eternal life, rather than eternal punishment. We wanted them to know, the choice was their's to make.

We had brought a guitar, and our Trumpeter had brought his horns. We gathered in a front of a small Arab shop off to one side of the Square. We sang songs of worship and praise, a bit off key, but none the less, we sang. As people came by, we gave them something to read about Jesus, and talked to those who would listen.

An hour into our fun, an American came and stopped in front of us. I approached him and struck up a conversation. I learned that he was in charge of a Camera News Team for ABC Television from the United States. After learning what we were doing, he asked if he could bring his crew and film some of our activity. I welcomed him to do so.

When he returned with his crew, an Israeli Television crew was following them. Both Camera crews filmed us at some length as we sang in worship, blew the trumpet, and shared with others about Jesus. The next day our phone was buzzing. Several of our Israeli friends had seen us on local television. Not something many Christians want in Israel. To be seen witnessing was bad enough, but to be filmed and shown on the air, that was another thing. We saw it quite differently. What a welcome gift, to air us telling others about Jesus. All the more exposure for our Lord.

Days later, by telephone call to the U.S., my Pastor told me that someone thought they had seen me on Television. Another report came later saying the same thing. God had taken a small band of believers who were radical enough to risk looking foolish, and aired their message of the gospel to at least two countries, maybe more.

Easter morning arrived, and our alarm clock sang out in the darkness. I looked at the red digital numerals and saw that it was

2:00 A.M. By 2:30, Maureen was waving goodbye to me from the door. I waited on the curb, and soon, David and Margaret pulled alongside and I jumped in. David was the Trumpeter, and Margaret played the guitar, in Manger Square at Christmas eve. We were on our way to the Old City of Jerusalem. Our aim was to pray as we walked around the outside of the walls, stop at every Gate, and as David blew the trumpet, we would Praise and Worship our Lord. About thirty came in the darkness of this early hour, and we spent the next two hours walking, praying, singing, and simply rejoicing around the walls of ancient Jerusalem.

At sunup we completed the march around the city, just in time to make our way to the nearby Garden Tomb. Easter services would be held every two hours in different languages throughout the day. We crowded into the Garden, and I stood a short distance from the Tomb itself. Two thousand years ago, the rock had been rolled away from the entrance of the Tomb, and Jesus rose and began appearing to many. There was great reason for us to sing His praises this morning. He indeed lives.

A few months earlier, Maureen and I had sat within fifteen feet of this same Tomb entrance, as several thousand gathered at midnight on the last night of the millennium, New Year's Eve. Around the world people were afraid of what might happen when Year 2000 sprang forth, Y2K. Fear circled the globe. Many moved families into the mountains, others filled storerooms with supplies and water. And in Israel much fear was also present. Some thought that pandemonium would erupt, and the streets would be filled with terror and fighting over water and supplies.

We chose to believe otherwise, and knew that if we were wrong, we could find no place better to be, than praising and worshiping our Lord in Jerusalem. If there was to be trouble, why not be in the midst of it, where our witness may help someone. Our rejoicing could be heard beyond the walls of this peaceful Garden

111

Tomb, as thousands of us raised our voices heavenward. And there was to be no terror.

For nine months in Jerusalem, I had enjoyed a new way of life. God had made major changes in both my life, and Maureen's. Now it was becoming clear that God was directing us to leave. Daily quiet times were the order of business in our home, our way of knowing what God desires of us. It was during one of these times He spoke that we were to go to Boulder City, Nevada, and gave us the exact date to do so.

We weren't sure why God would take us from Israel to Nevada, but knew that His reasons were good enough for us. We thrilled in hearing Him ask something of us. It was another opportunity to obey.

Because Maureen was not an American, a stop at the American Embassy in the Arab controlled, East Jerusalem, was necessary. I had been in other American Embassies and thought I knew what to expect. I had been treated like royalty in Calcutta, just a couple years earlier. I had been in Embassies of Canada, South Africa, and India. None compared with how we American's were treated in our own embassy, the best.

But, this time it would be different. I had to stand on the sidewalk in foul weather to conduct business. I stood in line with the many Arab, and Israeli's, who wanted to go to America. I didn't mind that at all, it only seemed fair, but inside I found that things were not on the up and up. By the time we had made multiple trips to acquire an Immigration Visa application for Maureen, the corruptness began to show through. There were moves that made me think that bribery hints were being made. When I went to the Lord with my concerns, He spoke very clearly to cancel the application.

I made a special trip to the East Jerusalem Embassy to do just that. I was taken through three levels of authority, and at each, threatened that if we did cancel, Maureen had no chance of getting to America. In fact, if we ever did get there, they would send her straight back to South Africa without issuing any sort of Visa.

I stood at the counter looking into the eyes of the third level supervisor who was now to persuade me differently. He had stood in the background and eavesdropped while I talked to the first two. I knew in my heart it was time to take a stand. Jesus was asking me not to be intimidated, and to take a stand for righteousness. I knew too, if I offered a bribe at this point the application process would begin to go smoothly. However, I had no inclination to do so.

This supervisor spoke, "What's the problem, Mr. Williamson?"

I said, "Please cancel our application." The supervisor got very angry and continued the argument of the previous two. He accused me of being unwise. I told him I didn't want to be unwise and would think about it for a couple days before canceling. I truly did not want to be unwise, or act foolishly. I wanted to hear exactly what my Lord was saying.

After praying a couple days, I knew more than ever I was supposed to cancel. I asked the Lord to go before me. I called the Embassy, and once the right person was on the phone, I said, "Please cancel our application for Maureen's Immigration."

After a few questions, the gentleman said, "It will be taken care in the hour, Mr. Williamson."

That was done, but Maureen still needed a Visa to go to the United States. We had been to the American Embassy in Tel Aviv on one other occasion, but had been told they could not help us because we lived in Jerusalem. We must use the East Jerusalem Embassy, where we had just canceled. We began to pray.

In the meantime, we had found a good Travel Agent and booked a May flight to the USA. We had no money for the tickets, nor did Maureen have a Visa, we were moving by faith. Faith that God would provide both the money for the flight, and the means for her Visa. I called the Embassy in Tel Aviv and explained that we lived in Jerusalem, were traveling to the USA, and needed a Visa for Maureen. The agent on the phone suggested the fastest way was to apply for the Visa through our Travel Agent.

We returned to Promised Land Ltd. on Hilliel Street. Our agent was reluctant to send Maureen's Visa application through the Embassy in Tel Aviv because her office had always dealt with East Jerusalem, and they were actually required to do so. I suggested she call the Tel Aviv Embassy for permission to send it there. She called, and the answer was, "No!'

After an hour of discussion, I told her I would write a letter to the Tel Aviv American Embassy explaining our reasons for applying there. She could attach my statement with the application. I urged her to call again. She did so reluctantly, this time there was a favorable reply, "Send it to us, we'll take a look at it."

I did write the letter, and told the truth as I knew it to be. I told of the circumstances surrounding our application at the East Jerusalem Embassy, the threats, and subsequent cancellation. I then requested a long term, multiple entry, Visitor's Visa to the United States, for Maureen.

Only ten days before our departure flight, and we were just now sending the Visa application by snail mail to Tel Aviv. It was thought to require about five days for the process. Our agent thought there to be little chance they would process it in Tel Aviv at all. It may be rejected and sent back. The situation did not look good.

God's hand had turned for us in many eleventh hour situations, however. This would be no exception. One week before our scheduled flight to America, I was in the home of a brother and sister in Christ in the heart of Jerusalem. The phone rang, Martha came to me and said, "It's for you, Bill."

I walked down the narrow hallway to the wall phone, picked up the receiver, and said, "Hello."

Maureen's voice sounded with some excitement. "Our travel agent called, the American Embassy gave me a ten year, multiple entry, Visa."

I couldn't contain myself, I screeched, "Yes!" and shot my one free hand into the air. At that moment the hallway door sprang open and the flash of Martha's camera momentarily blinded me. She had captured me at the height of my celebration.

It was with great joy that we returned to Promised Land Ltd. to pick up our airline tickets, and Maureen's passport, now stamped with the ten year visa. Our travel agent was thrilled, and proclaimed that she had indeed seen a miracle. She said, "The one you serve, is a mighty God."

In East Jerusalem, intimidation and fear tactics had been used against us. But we had not succumb to fear. We heard our Lord when He said, "Take a stand." Once we heard, we then obeyed.

Throughout my Christian walk, there has often been doubt that I was hearing rightly. "Is that really you, God?" was often my cry. One morning during my quiet time in Jerusalem, I felt a strong message from my God, "I am NOT taking you to new levels of hearing my voice, I'm taking you to new levels of believing what you hear."

May 24th came, and as we lifted off the runway at Ben Gurion International in Tel Aviv, I glanced toward the American Embassy, and wondered who God had touched on our behalf. We were headed to America. "Thank you, Lord."

Chapter 13

Bi Bi, My Forever Friend

Written by: Maureen and Bill Williamson

On a pretty couch in Jerusalem, I sat with my dear sister in Christ, Chana. Jewish by birth, she had a glorious conversion, and now lives to worship and serve Jesus Christ with a full knowledge of her Jewish roots. Chana is the epitome of what is called today, a Messianic Jew, or Messianic Believer. A born again, Child of God.

Chana and I were browsing through her photo albums. Throughout the photos from a young age, a very beautiful lady showed up. "Who is this lovely lady?" I enquired.

"Oh that's, BiBi Hilton," Chana proudly said. "She is my dearest friend. She is married to Eric Hilton, son of Conrad Hilton, of the worldwide Hilton Hotel chain. BiBi is also related to Elizabeth Taylor, who was a Hilton herself once upon a time when she married Nick Hilton, her first husband."

"Wow!" I said, "Do you think I could meet such a beautiful lady?"

"No, not likely," Chana said, "BiBi and I were childhood friends, she now lives in Las Vegas, Nevada. I do not see you going to Las Vegas, do you?"

"No, probably not," I said, "but maybe she will come and visit you here in Israel, and then we could meet."

"Maybe," Chana said.

"Las Vegas," I dreamed, "What a wonderland. Maybe the Lord will take me there one day." I thrilled at the thought.

But for now, back to reality. Bill entered my single life of twenty years, and suddenly everything was different. Now I was married to an American, and the Lord was speaking to us about leaving my beloved Israel to live in the United States. The Lord showed us it was Boulder City, Nevada that he had called us to, and my first question was, "Is Boulder City anywhere near Las Vegas?"

"Just twenty minutes by freeway," replied Bill.

Immediately, in my minds eye, I saw the beautiful red headed lady I had admired in Chana's photo album. "Hallelujah, Lord! You are going to make a way for us to meet BiBi Hilton, but how, Lord?" I wondered.

Leaving my beloved Israel was an enormous adjustment, but the Lord had brought revelation and understanding in His Word through Proverbs 3:5-6, *'Trust in the LORD with all thine heart; and lean not unto thine own understanding. In all thy ways acknowledge him, and he shall direct thy paths.'* God had truly blessed me with a wonderful American husband and we were going to America.

My Jerusalem friend, Chana was excited for us and asked if I would carry, and deliver, a tiny jewelry gift to her friend, BiBi in Las Vegas.

"It's that beautiful lady isn't it?" I enquired.

"Hallelujah yes," said Chana, "God has heard your prayer."

Soon the time came for our departure, and we had everything we possessed in two large suitcases and two carry-on bags. We arrived at Ben Gurion International Airport at Tel Aviv and found it the usual hub of activity . It was not unusual for Christians to be singled out in Israel for inspection at the airport, especially if they were particularly outspoken about their faith, and this time would be no exception.

My husband and I had been talking to a young Jewish man about Jesus. He was returning to England after working on a Kibbutz for a period of months. We, nor he, had noticed the check-in area open to travelers. Consequently, we were at the very end of the line that had quickly formed into the check-in area. Suddenly, Bill and I were summoned forward and escorted past even the first in line. We were asked questions about who we knew in Israel, where we were going, and when we would be back. We were then required to open our suitcases.

We're accustomed to this kind of treatment and politely agreed. Nothing in the bags concerned the officer until he discovered the tiny, brightly wrapped gift for BiBi. He picked it up,

119

looked at us and said, "What is this?" I explained it was simply a gift from a friend in Israel, to another friend in America. "What's inside?" he continued in his broken English. I explained that we had not seen it wrapped, and was not sure what it was.

The officer walked away with the tiny package held in front of him, muttering something about x-ray. It wasn't long before he returned with the package and handed it to me. We quickly zipped the bags closed, and we were off to check in. Thank you, Lord, for bringing us to the front of the line. Persecution does have benefit at times.

I telephoned BiBi shortly after we settled in America. I was delighted to find out that Chana had told BiBi quite a bit about my life of living by faith, and my marriage to an equally sold out Christian.

The day came when BiBi invited us to meet her and a few acquaintances that were interested in meeting missionaries from Jerusalem. BiBi set up our lunch meeting at her Country Club at Spanish Trails.

With our directions to the Hilton's Country Club in our hands we set out for Las Vegas. Our car was a 1988 Plymouth Mini-Van with more than 250,000 miles on it. It smoked when accelerating, and ran very hot because of a poor cooling system. On this particular day the temperature was 115 degrees, with no relief in sight. The air-conditioner had failed several days earlier. We had put on our 'Sunday best' clothes and by the time we were a few miles from home we were cooked with our 'Sunday best' sticking to us.

Because the cooling system was not adequate, we carried extra containers of water in the van. But, on this day we ran out of water in route. We were forced to pull into a gas station just before arriving at Spanish Trails, and spray water on the radiator to cool it down.

We arrived at one of the front gates of Spanish Trails, and rolled to a stop. The security officer looked us over from front to back before addressing us. He obviously hadn't seen too many cars like ours come through 'his' gates. All the paint was missing off the car's hood and roof, and some of the simulated wood grain paneling had peeled off the sides. The heat from the overheated engine was radiating in all directions, and a bit of blue smoke curled up from the tailpipe. He gave us a rather smug, "Yes?"

And Bill said, "We're here to see Eric Hilton." BiBi had instructed us to say that.

The security officer looked down his nose at us, and said, "Who?"

Bill repeated, "We're here to meet with, Eric Hilton."

The officer turned to his computer and began scanning for anything giving him a clue as to who we were. He found nothing, at least his face indicated that, as he turned back to us. Bill offered more information, "We were asked to meet him at the Country Club."

He straightened himself and said, "You're at the wrong gate for the Country Club. The gate you're looking for is about a mile in that direction." And he pointed.

We thanked him, and circled his security station with 'ole blue' to reverse direction, I'm sure leaving a strong odor of overheated Plymouth Voyager behind. We received much the same treatment when we arrived at the proper gate, but were found on the computer. We were issued the proper insignia to hang upon our rear view mirror, and warned to stay only to the exact route to the Club.

We pulled into the parking lot of the Club and parked some distance from the entrance so as not to embarrass the club with our 'Beverly Hillbillies' style limo. The sign at the Valet entrance read,

"Tow Away Zone." Bill smiled, and said, "That sign is especially for us." We laughed, and tried to straighten our very hot, sticky clothing.

The foyer of the Club was very nice, and refreshingly cool with a lavish fountain spraying water high into the air towards the domed ceiling. Bill signaled to a lone Club worker, and he came to us. Bill told him we were looking for Eric Hilton. At that, he stepped over a short distance and pointed beyond a partition to three men sitting at the far end of the lounge. There was no one else in the place. Bill and I boldly walked to the table, and Bill spoke to the three men. "Eric Hilton?" Eric looked up, and Bill directed his words to him, "I'm Bill Williamson, and this is my wife, Maureen."

Eric stood, extended his hand, and said, "I think you're looking for my wife."

Bill said, as they shook hands, "Yes, we are."

Eric pointed in the direction of BiBi and explained where to find her. We turned to go and met BiBi face to face as she glided into the room. There was no doubt who this was. She was dressed in a beautiful flowing white ensemble, including the hat. BiBi was very elegant and her very presence demanded attention. She looked like a wonderful blend of an angel and Mother Superior.

BiBi's smile was full and warm. She greeted us, and then led us to the dining section she had come from, where three of her companions were seated. BiBi introduced us, and we sat down.

The dining area of the Country Club was also deserted, except for the six of us at this rather large round table. It's as though Eric and BiBi had the entire Club to themselves. Something cool to drink was ordered, and Bill and I exchanged conversation with BiBi as the others talked amongst themselves momentarily.

Finally one of the other three guests asked where we were living. Upon hearing Boulder City, another asked, "Why, Boulder City?"

Bill and I looked at each other to see which of us would field that particular question. We knew that this was an opening to speak the gospel of Jesus Christ. Our lives are dedicated to nothing less than Jesus Christ and Him crucified. We cannot talk about where we are, where we are going, or what we are doing, without talking about Jesus. He is our everything.

I smiled at Bill, and he turned and spoke, "We came in response to the Lord's request. He asked us to come."

"You mean God speaks directly to you like you're someone special?" was the next question.

Bill wasted no time, "Yes, He does speak directly to us."

The next enquiry was on the lips waiting for opportunity, "How does He speak to you? Like we're speaking now?"

Bill continued, "Jesus told us in John 10:27, *'My sheep hear my voice, and I know them, and they follow me.'* God is not limited, but can speak to us anyway He chooses. However, with me, He most often speaks in a still, small voice. I must be quiet before Him, and listen. I spend time each day just listening, as well as praying and reading the Bible, His Word. It isn't enough to just listen though," Bill went on, "I must be living my life the way He desires me to. He desires us to live free of sin, and have a desire to know Him more."

"What do you do in Boulder City?" came the next question.

"Bill volunteers in the church office doing administrative things, and I keep our communication center going at home," I said.

"What kind of church do you belong to? I've seen some of those radical ones where everyone is waving their hands in the air."

"That's us," Bill cheerfully announced. "We're sometimes in churches where no one raises their hands, but we prefer to attend where it is acceptable. Raising hands is just another way of

Praising Jesus. He is worth praising because of all that He has done for us. We love to express our love and thankfulness to Him visibly. We're glad to be radical for Jesus."

Another of the guest's offered, "I like the idea of reincarnation. What are your thoughts on this subject?"

Bill said, "We don't believe in reincarnation, we believe in resurrection! The Bible says in Hebrews 9:27, '....*it is appointed unto men once to die, but after this the judgment.'* We don't have to come back and endure another life on this planet through reincarnation. Jesus went to the cross and died, yes. But, He also rose from the grave in three days, death could not hold Him. He said one day He will return to judge the earth. Those who accept Him, believe in Him, shall join Him for eternity. Those who do not, shall perish. It says in John 3:16-17, *'For God so loved the world, that he gave his only begotten Son, that whosoever believeth in him should not perish, but have everlasting life. For God sent not his Son into the world to condemn the world; but that the world through him might be saved"*

Bill continued, "Jesus took on the sins of the world when He went to the cross and chose to die for us, in our place. We deserve eternal death, but by His grace we escape and have eternal life instead. He died that we might live. We believe because of Jesus Christ, we will be with Him in heaven for eternity, once this brief time on earth is finished. If we should die before He returns for us, then scripture says that we will be caught up from the grave to join Him in the clouds. All of this happens because of His great love for us."

We were then asked, "If all you do is listen to God, and do what you're told, how do you live? How do you pay your bills?"

I spoke this time, "God has promised those who trust in Him and seek to serve Him with all their hearts, minds and souls, that their every need will be met. He will provide totally for those who put their trust in Him. Jesus himself said in Matt 6:31-33, *'Therefore take no thought, saying, What shall we eat? or, What shall we drink? or, Wherewithal shall we be clothed? (For after all these things do the Gentiles seek:) for your heavenly Father knoweth that ye have need of all these things. But seek ye first the kingdom of God, and his righteousness; and all these things shall be added unto you.'* We travel the world in obedience to Him, and we have no money, or substantial income. God provides everything as we need it."

Bill added, "Sometimes we do work at a regular paying job, but only after we know God is asking us to do so. He is the key, what does He say?"

I said, "I'd love for you to come to our lovely home and see all the delightfully coordinated furnishings God has provided for us, at little or no cost."

A final question came forth, "How does God give you the money you need?"

"Mostly through believers," Bill answered. "God puts our need upon someone's heart, and the funds required are provided. We're not talking about wants, but needs. Sometimes food is scarce, often we must wait until the eleventh hour before the need is met. But we grow in faith each time He faithfully provides. He has never let us down, He is trustworthy. We simply focus on obeying His every command and request He makes of us, He takes care of the rest."

The conversation turned to the many places we had lived in our lives as God moves us around. And one lady asked, "Isn't it hard to always leave your friends behind?"

I told her, "That's why we have a communication center in our home. We are in contact with hundreds of people all around the world. We don't lose the friends, we simply add them to our list. And it's not unusual to see them again as we go around this globe serving Jesus."

At that point, I turned to BiBi and said, "You must also have many wonderful and close friends."

There was a moment of poignant stillness before she said, "What do you mean, close friend?"

I said, "Someone you trust, someone you can confide in, and someone who cares deeply for you."

It was at this moment that I decided to be BiBi's 'forever friend.' BiBi's eyes looked pensive, even a hint of a tear, as she said, "No, there is no one like that."

I understood, and I believe it must be difficult to have real friends in the circles that BiBi and Eric move in. People most often come to them with their hands out, seeking something from them. Bill and I do not come to them with our hands out, but come only with friendship, and a message our desperate world needs to hear. Sadly, many are dying eternally without hearing it. Those who hear, and believe, will not perish but have everlasting life. The Word tells us that! We bring this truth to all who will listen.

As we talked with BiBi, she showered us with gifts that kept coming out of her handbag. It was easy to see that BiBi had a very kind heart, and a generous one.

Eventually we moved away from the dining table, and strolled about the Club as BiBi pointed out some particularly nice art work. We stepped out onto the lovely shaded patio, and a few extravagant houses were pointed out. Some valued at eight million dollars.

Back inside we made our way past the fountain to the entrance. We expected to be left at this point so we could retreat to our smudgy old mini van. But to our surprise, all of them followed us out into the heat that was blistering Las Vegas that day. We chatted as we crossed the parking lot to where we had parked. We said our goodbyes, and fired up 'ole blue.' Blue smoke once again belched out of the exhaust pipe as we backed up, and then pulled past the four of them. They stood near the gate of the Country Club as we went through and turned toward the Security Station. The four of them stood waving to us as we pulled away.

The sweat began to pour from us once again as we turned onto Tropicana and sped toward the Strip, and beyond, to our cozy little home in Boulder City. It all seemed like a dream to us. How could two missionaries like us have ever orchestrated an afternoon like this without God's love wanting to reach out to these very precious people. We knew that God had something for BiBi and Eric, and that He may carry it to them through us. We feel very privileged.

It's some time now and we see God's hand in the forming of this friendship with BiBi and Eric. We pray that we can continue to shower them with God's love. We pray too, they will acknowledge the way we spend eternity, involves a choice.

It was worth the coming to America, just to meet you, BiBi. And just as you are my 'forever friend,' this is a 'forever story,' there is no end to it.

Chapter 14

Build My Church

Written by: Bill Williamson

Maureen and I stepped out of the Las Vegas airport terminal, and the night air hit us in the face with a suffocating affect. "How could it be this hot after dark," I commented. All of our Jerusalem possessions now reduced to just two suitcases and our carry on luggage, we searched for our shuttle bus.

Tel Aviv, London, Los Angeles, and now Las Vegas, all behind us; we drove a rented car toward Boulder City, only thirty minutes from the airport. The magnificent lights of Las Vegas looked like a sea of orange glass in our rearview mirror. Maureen, exhausted, was slumped in her seat. The trip had been long; two days from Jerusalem to Boulder City, Nevada.

Three days later jet lag was taking its toll, but none the less, we were happy to be where God had directed us. He had spoken specifically, "Come to Boulder City." Furthermore, He said, "Build My Church." We were uncertain what that meant, but had come to a 'storefront church' in obedience, to do so.

We leased a condo at a good price, and moved in with only our luggage. God began doing miracles daily, and furnishings came from many sources. We had come with nothing, but the Lord quickly filled our condo, and we were on our way to making it a home. A very tasteful one at that; with Maureen's special touch.

A group from our new church turned up on our doorstep one evening. Items were piled in our kitchen until there was no more room on the counters, or in the refrigerator. Gift certificates, checks, and cash was brought. They had come to say, "Welcome." We saw the 'Body of Christ' in action, and it was beautiful.

One precious saint came for Maureen one morning, took her to a fabulous store where Maureen could shop to her heart's content for silk flowers. Margaret turned Maureen loose and said, "Go for it, I've got $150.00."

Many left blessings at our door, or at the church, without recognition. They were silently showing us Jesus.

One of our church leadership owns an Auto Repair Shop. George kept our car running for a year and a half, at very little cost to us.

The car is another story altogether. 'Ole Blue' we came to call it, was a twelve year old Plymouth Voyager, a mini van. Pastor

130

and his wife presented it to us upon arrival, as a gift. 'Ole Blue' had traveled a quarter of a million miles of streets and highways. My first thought was, "It won't make it long, how can it?" After another 20,000 miles 'Ole Blue' still curled a bit of blue smoke from the tailpipe, but had been faithful.

But, let's back up a little. After two weeks in the States we had moved into our condo. We soon had a few modest furnishings, but our cupboards were literally bare, and our refrigerator contained only a half a lemon, and a glass of milk. We had survived on six potatoes for three days.

For days we had been seeking God about our reason for being here in Boulder City. We knew He had brought us to, 'Build His Church,' but we knew that 'opportunity' doesn't mean 'calling.' In other words, we weren't supposed to do just anything that came along. We determined to know what God meant by, "Build My Church."

The Lord spoke repeatedly from His Word, "Willingly serve, present yourselves." I called Pastor and asked to meet him. We were soon sitting at the edge of the desert in his Ford Ranger pickup. It was good to be back with my Pastor and friend.

Pastor and his family had answered the specific call of God five years earlier while Pastor of a wonderful congregation in Central Oregon. They left behind a Christian School, Church, home, and many friends, to come to the Southern Nevada desert and plant a church. They had responded with a hearty, 'Yes, Lord,' but it hadn't been easy. Finally they had acquired a 'storefront' location that would serve as home for the congregation. Moving equipment in on Saturdays, and out on Sundays, like they had done for two years would no longer be required.

Pastor looked across the seat at me and asked, "What's on your mind, Bill?"

131

I told him what the Lord had been showing me, and that I was willing to serve however he needed. Pastor welcomed the offer, and explained the need for administrative help in the office and accounting areas. I agreed to serve in both areas. Note I said, 'serve,' not 'work.' I differentiate because I had been offered salaried positions is the past. I had even inquired of the Lord about seeking work. He always said to me, "You have work. You are in my employment." I had not come to this 'storefront church' for a salary. God is our salary.

At our moment of commitment to this 'storefront church,' something happened in the heavenly realm. Food items came in that day, and we received several hundred dollars from two unexpected sources. God had once again opened the floodgates of His provision, and it progressed to avalanche proportion during our time here. I believe He was waiting to see if we would serve in this 'storefront church.' And would we 'willingly serve,' even if our cupboards and pockets were empty?

Just as Jesus came to serve, in His own words, we too must serve. That's one way of 'Building His Church.'

God wants to use this 'storefront church' to raise up a standard here in the desert. This area of Nevada is steeped in darkness. Gambling, and all the related corruptness, dominates the economy. Las Vegas and Henderson is touted to be the fastest growing area in the nation, and has been on this run for more than ten years. People are moving from all parts of the U.S. It's said that five thousand people a month are relocating to Las Vegas area. I wonder how many people are leaving, broke and disillusioned.

The size of this 'storefront church' is slight, but the work is mighty. God is establishing a 'Light' in this dark land. Why do I say this? Let me explain.

Several years ago, in the months before I had gone to Israel, Pastor and I were often at the church, sometimes into the night, doing remodeling work. One particular evening I was torn between working on my newly acquired apartment, or working on the church. It occurred to me that I could work two hours in the church, and still get home early enough to work on my place too. I changed into work clothes and left for the church.

After thirty minutes of work, a voice spoke and I was startled. I thought I was alone in the building. I stepped into the hallway, met him face to face, and he spoke again, "What time are your services?"

His name was James, and he worked for the carnival that had just arrived in town. Over the next hour and some minutes, James told me his story.

He was saved seventeen years ago. His father died of heart failure shortly after that. He was the victim of sodomy, and raped at eleven. He ran, lived on the streets, and became addicted to crack. He was introduced to a Christian Ministry called, Teen Challenge, and was set free from drugs. He'd been off drugs ten years.

James met a girl from Detroit and they married. James' wife gave birth to twins. When the twins were five years old, she stopped by a market to buy soft drinks. When she came out of the market, she stepped into a dispute between two men. Guns appeared, shots were fired, she was dead. James lost his children to her parents in a custody battle. James joined a traveling carnival show.

James didn't like carnival life. He was running away, mostly from God. And he knew God was pursuing him. Finally, James said, "I don't even know why I came over here. I was at the grocery store across the street, and when I came out, I noticed this church. It appeared as a lighthouse. It was so bright in a sea of darkness, I just had to come over."

At these words my eyes began to water. There were no bright lights coming from the building, only a hall light. James had seen a supernatural light. During recent prayer times I had seen this building as a place where God's light was going forth to Boulder City. Others had specifically seen it as a 'Lighthouse' to the entire Las Vegas area.

I gave James encouragement in his walk. We prayed together, hugged, and he agreed to stop running from God. He stepped into the darkness, and was gone. I never saw James again. But, I did see what God wanted us at this 'storefront church' to see, and He had sent a carnival worker to show us. This 'storefront church' was in fact, a 'Lighthouse.' He would draw many to Him through it.

Millions of cars pass this 'storefront church' every year, and most come to Las Vegas with intent to dip into the darkness, not knowing the harm that it can bring. He placed this 'Lighthouse' along the path so that many might see.

The darkness was never quite so evident as it was when Avivah visited us from Jerusalem. We talked of the marvelous lights, the extravagant casino designs, and the various shows that can be seen from the streets in Las Vegas. We decided to take our guest for a tour.

We were in a festive mood as we piled into 'Ole Blue' and headed for Las Vegas. We drove through Railroad Pass, located in a range of desert mountains that separate Boulder City and Las Vegas, and we could see the sea of lights that awaited us. The excitement mounted as we drew closer. One mile remained on Interstate 215 before we would pull off onto Las Vegas Boulevard, commonly known as, 'The Strip.'

As I drove, I suddenly felt a hush come over me. I instantly knew something was wrong. Maureen and Avivah continued a discussion. A heaviness persisted. I whispered to my God, "What is it, Lord?" I slowed 'Ole Blue' some, and pressed again, "What is it, Lord?" I received no response.

A moment later I knew that we must stop and pray. I made the exit onto 'The Strip,' and noticed a wide dirt area to the right. At this point we were still outside the lighted area of 'The Strip.' I abruptly pulled into the wide area, stopped, and turned off the engine and lights. Maureen and Avivah, a bit surprised, turned to me. I said, "We've got to pray, something's wrong."

I quicky explained, and we began to pray. We repented for our festive attitude and asked Father to show us the truth. I looked through the windshield at the brightly lit Las Vegas ahead. The glitter and sparkle began to take on a different look. I instinctively felt I was looking into the gates of a tremendous stronghold of our enemy, Satan. I saw that all that glittered there was not good, but that it was cover for evil. I saw that thousands came from all over the world to partake of it freely. I saw that the 'beauty' had nothing to offer but death. We prayed against the stronghold in Jesus name.

We continued on into the bright lights and glittering hype of Las Vegas. However, our attitude was quite different. We prayed for those we saw wondering aimlessly along 'The Strip.' We prayed against the workings of the enemy of our souls in the casinos we drove by. Our festive mood had turned into one of somber intercession for the city, and the people.

This journey along 'The Strip' was some time ago, but Maureen and I still view Las Vegas the same today. We know there is great need in Las Vegas, but let's remember, Romans 5:20 *".....But where sin abounded, grace did much more abound."*

The real light is not on 'The Strip,' but in places like this small 'storefront church' along a crowded highway. It's a 'wide road,' but God has placed His Lighthouse's to help turn people onto the 'Narrow Road.' Matthew 7:13-14 says, *"Enter by the narrow gate; for wide is the gate and broad is the way that leads to destruction, and there are many who go in by it. Because narrow is the gate and difficult is the way which leads to life, and there are few who find it."*

One such example of the drawing power of the Light of God is seen in, Rick. It was a Sunday night when we gathered in the 'storefront church' for worship, and something from the Word. Rick came in during the singing, and I turned to look at him. He looked like a man who had seen a ghost. He appeared in shock, and in agony. He sat at the back of the church. After some moments Pastor asked if he was alright. There was little indication from Rick's hanging head. Pastor ask us to extend our hands to him, and he began to pray. Rick began to sob uncontrollably. I rose to my feet, as did Ron, another of our dear saints, and moved back to where Rick was.

Ron and I stood with Rick, our hands on him in support, praying. We prayed, and he confessed in repentance, crying out to the Lord for forgiveness.

Rick had been a faithful Christian at one point in his life, but had turned back to drugs and left the fellowship of believers. He had forsaken the way of the Lord. This very night Rick had come to the doors of this 'storefront church' and stood. There he battled to enter. All that was wrong inside wanted to run away, but something was compelling him to come in. He later said that pushing through that door had been one of the hardest things he had ever done. I don't think Rick was aware, at that moment he had been fighting for his life.

I believe the Light of Christ drew him in, and because he did push through, victory came to him through that same Jesus. Today, Rick is whole and healthy, with drugs far behind him, and he is faithful in attendance at the 'storefront church.' Rick has a weekly gathering of saints meeting in his home. Rick responded to the 'Light' of this 'Desert Lighthouse,' and now he is affecting others to the Glory of God.

My dear wife, Maureen, has written two previous books telling of people like Rick she has encountered over the past twenty years. She mostly gives the books away to encourage others, and to let the power of God, through Jesus Christ, be known. Her second book, 'Assignment Love,' had been in the hands of her publisher in Johannesburg, South Africa when that same publisher filed bankruptcy. They had published it, marketed it, and now held one thousand of the books in their warehouse.

We had been in America a few months when we received communication from the publisher. They were selling off the remaining books at a discount price, and offered Maureen first chance at purchase. Our desire was to have the books in our possession for use in evangelism. The purchase price to us was just over one U.S. dollar per book, a thousand dollars. We committed to the purchase, believing God approved.

A shipping company was found in Cape Town that would ship them to Las Vegas for about five hundred dollars, making the total cost of the books, fifteen hundred dollars. Not a lot of money, but we had none. We began to pray for the money to come in.

Over the next several months we put money away at every opportunity, forgoing groceries, gas, or other essentials, in order that the 'book fund' would grow. Some of our brothers and sisters in Christ responded with financial gifts, and soon the books were on their way.

There is now a continual flow of these books going out of our home. Anyone who shows an interest receives one. It doesn't matter if they are down the street, or half way around the world. Our postage costs averaged sixty dollars a month the first six months of that year. Communicating Jesus is a major part of our life and ministry.

Shortly after the books arrived, we put a plan in place to go 'door to door' and visit our eighty-three neighbors in our condo complex. Over a period of six weeks we knocked on every door. When our knock was answered, we told them we were new to the complex, and wanted them to know that Jesus loves them. Along with the book, we gave them a poem called, 'Voice From Hell,' and a letter we composed explaining our commitment to Jesus Christ, and everyone's need of Him to ensure eternal life.

We had great fun with this 'door to door' project. We were met at the door by some dripping with shower water, wrapped only in towels. Some were clad in housecoats, rubbing sleep from their eyes. Many work nights in the 24 hour city of Las Vegas. We were prepared for that. We carried an attractively decorated handbag with a number of packets to be given away that particular day. Each packet contained the book, poem, and letter. The packet was addressed to our neighbor, labeled, "From your neighbor in 17B." When no one answered our knock, we leaned the packet against their door.

One night as we left our unit for our evening walk, one of our nearest neighbors ran along the sidewalk and approached us from behind. She thanked us for the book, and began to tell us something about herself. She had great need for prayer, and we could see, it was now that she needed it. We asked if we could pray. She eagerly agreed, and the three of us grasped hands right there on the sidewalk, and lifted her need to the Lord. Tears were present, but a peace came to Teresa at that moment. Our relationship continued to grow as we met and prayed together.

Most of the other neighbors had friendly waves when they saw us after that. Before, we were just another unknown quantity that had moved in, now we were the neighbors who reached out in love. Surely God is using the book, the poem, or the letter, to bring attention to His Son, Jesus, in their lives, or lives of family and friends. There had been a great price to bring the books from Africa, but there will be great reward too.

We had discovered another way that God wanted to, "Build His Church."

Maureen and I are so impressed with the poem, 'Voice From Hell,' we include it here for you to read. Let the words, and meaning, 'soak in' and see what they compel you to do.

A Voice From Hell

You lived next door to me for years;
We shared our dreams, our joys, and tears.
A friend to me you were indeed...
A friend who helped me when in need.

My faith in you was strong and sure;
We had such trust as should endure.
No spats between us ever arose;
Our friends were alike....and so our foes.

What sadness then, my friend, to find
That after all, you weren't so kind.
The day my life on earth did end,
I found you weren't a faithful friend.

For all those years we spent on earth,
You never talked of second birth.
You never spoke of my lost soul
And of the Messiah who'd make me whole.

I plead today from Hell's cruel fire

And tell you now my last desire.
You cannot do a thing for me...
No words today my bonds will free.

But do not err, my friend, again;
Do all you can for souls of men.
Plead with them now quite earnestly,
Lest they be cast in Hell with me.

Author Unknown....

During another daily quiet time with my Lord, He spoke the words, "Proverbs Project." Odd, I thought, because we had been considering having a home Bible study focusing on the Book of Proverbs.

The basic premise of the 'Proverbs Project' would be to, read a chapter of Proverbs every week for thirty-one weeks, until the thirty-one chapters were finished. We would read that week's chapter daily during the week leading up to the home meeting. And during each meeting we would discuss the gems, and questions, we had found while dwelling in the chapter day after day. Also in the meeting we would outline the new 'Project' for the coming week.

We promoted Proverbs Project at the 'storefront church,' and found interest. Zero interest would have been enough, as Maureen and I knew that God wanted us to conduct these meetings. It wasn't conditional upon how many would come. We vowed to do it, if no one else came. And on one occasion, we did just that.

Below are four examples of weekly 'projects' that were assigned:

1. Listen ~ Sit quietly with the Lord daily and ask Him to speak, listen for five minutes without distraction. Learn to recognize His voice.

2. Love someone ~ Look for opportunity to show love to someone new every day of coming week. A neighbor, co-worker, family member, or a stranger in town.

3. Ask Father daily for His loving Conviction, Rebuke, or Chastening. It is sweet and we shouldn't hide from it. Cherish it, want it, seek it. It's life giving!

4. Watch for lies, exaggerations, stretching the truth. Confess, admit, apologize, repent, remove yourself from it. Change!

There were thirty-one such 'projects.'

Our focus over the thirty-one weeks of Proverbs Project was to curb the tongue, avoid compromise, develop integrity, and practice reading the Bible daily. Maureen and I, as leaders, are convinced that we gained far more than any other as we spent time digging in Proverbs in preparation.

Again, we could see that God was using us to, "Build His Church." And, in the process, Maureen and I got built up also, because we too, are His Church.

Maureen and I drove into the desert one lovely Spring day, parked, and walked along a small ridge searching out the beauty of God's desert. We spied a small Barrel Cactus. It was beautiful with its hard, red tines sticking out all over its round green body. It was about the size of a cantaloupe, and would easily fit into one of our lovely house pots. We gathered it quite carefully, digging it out of the rocky soil. Once home, we potted it and proudly displayed it for all to see.

Over the many weeks of our Proverbs Project, we had talked of honesty, integrity, no compromise, and every aspect of walking out the Christian life. Upon the arrival of our regulars on Thursday night, several were quick to comment on our Barrel Cactus, and one said that it was illegal to dig desert plants in Nevada.

"We had broken the law!"

I wanted to immediately proclaim my ignorance, but I had suspected, when we dug the plant, that it may not be allowed. I went ahead figuring my ignorance was defense enough. Conviction fell upon me. I knew what we must do.

The next day I called the City Police. They informed me, "Yes, you have broken the law." I told them I would take the plant back and replant it exactly where I had taken it from. The dispatch officer was so impressed that I would actually call and ask, not to mention, a willingness to drive out to the desert and put it back, that she said, "If you'll take it back, that will be the end of the matter."

Maureen and I took the cactus, some water, digging tools, and drove out to the desert ridge in search of the hole the cactus had actually come from. We found it, replaced it tenderly, and marked the spot. Over the months we have returned to check on it, and found it has survived our compromise so far.

Is one cactus so important? Maybe not, but obedience is. I was disobedient when I dug the plant. Then, in repentance, I was obedient. Maureen and I take obedience that seriously. Obedience is important, but we must listen carefully first, lest we miss the instruction.

God was sharpening us by removing compromise. Again, 'Building His Church.'

When God said, "Come to Boulder City," and "Build My Church," we obeyed, and He always undertook for us in every way while serving there in the 'storefront church.' Every need was met, just as He promises us in His Word. He spoke, we heard, we obeyed, and He provided. That's the way it works. For us, it all starts with listening, and finishes with obedience.

In closing this chapter, I want to relate one more event that I have concluded, is 'Building His Church.'

My Pastor is so fervently after our Lord, it shows. He has been preaching from the pulpit for more than twenty-five years, and is 'earnestly contending for the faith.' He is a worshiper of God, and desires to see the Church revived.

During our time in Boulder City I had been sensing that more is needed from the pulpit, that God wants change in His church across the Western Hemisphere. I began to pray specifically about what it was, and how it applied to me. Even when I tried to divert my attention to other things I could not push the thoughts away. I wrote them down, thinking they were for some other time, some other place. But, I soon realized that they were for now, for my current church, for my Pastor.

In preparation for our upcoming move back to the Middle East I had terminated my service at the church. I was seeing my Pastor much less. We had been close for years and I missed seeing him. I called him, thinking only that the Lord wanted me to encourage him. Not far into our conversation, we talked of how we missed our frequent discussions, our breakfasts we used to have. We decided to get together on Wednesday for breakfast. For old times sake.

Wednesday came, and it was like old times. What a pleasure to sit across the table from my friend, and Pastor. I had not planned to talk about the things the Lord had shown me, unless of course, the Lord impressed it upon me.

The opportunity came and I knew it was right. I began to share in honesty, and bluntness. Pastor and I had always had this privilege in our relationship. God had often used each of us in the other's life, speaking truth, encouragement, exhortation, and sometimes even rebuke. Such is a true friendship between two born again believers.

In a nutshell, here's what I told him the Lord had placed on my heart for him, and the Church.

1. God desires 'His Voice' preached from the pulpit, and wants it to come directly from His throne. Not just a good message, but a specific Word from God for His specific people. My Pastor is a very gifted preacher. He can preach a message about anything he sees, hears, reads , or experiences. But maybe a message that is an 'Echo' of something besides God. God is looking for a 'Voice,' not an 'Echo.'

I felt to exhort my Pastor to spend more time with Father God, to receive input from the throne of God alone. People are hungry for manna from the Lord himself. If they don't receive it from the pulpit, the front door of the church will be revolving, with people leaving as fast as they come in. Maybe faster. Hungry, seeking people, are running from congregation to congregation looking for the 'Voice' of God. We often criticize those who do so, but maybe they are right, they simply aren't finding that 'Voice' they are looking for. Sadly, many churches are filled with complacent believers who want their ears tickled with an 'echo,' and even that must be done inside an hour's time.

If people are going to leave our churches, let it be for the reason of not being able to stand the intensity of what God is speaking through our Pastors. Let those who want their ears tickled, find it somewhere else.

2. Sarcasm is not acceptable from the pulpit. When I

felt I was to share this word, I wanted to know more about the word, 'sarcasm.' I went to my Oxford American Dictionary and found this definition: "Sarcasm' spoken is a, taunt." And, 'taunt,' is; "to jeer at, to try to provoke with scornful remarks or criticism."

It is right to 'provoke' the Body of Christ. I have felt recently the Lord exhorting me to be a 'provoker.' He wants me to exhort, even rebuke, in order to 'provoke' saints to acts that will glorify God. Acts that will sharpen integrity, honesty, and remove compromise from their lives. But, we have a choice in how we 'provoke,' and what we 'provoke' them to. Hebrews 10:24 says, *"And let us consider one another to provoke unto love and to good works."*

Let's provoke in a way that pleases the Creator of the Universe, our Lord.

3. God isn't seeking 'Secret Christians,' or 'secret salvation.' Salvation is one of the most amazing, spectacular events in our lives. Every Christian will confess that to be true. In our church, like so many, salvation almost seems a thing of shame in the way we present it. Everyone is required to lower their head. Their eyes must be closed. The one wanting salvation must only 'slip' his, or her hand up, so as not to be noticed, except by the Pastor. And then we must all pray aloud to cover the voice of the one receiving the most precious gift, eternal life. Once the conversion is made, then, and only then, can we open our eyes and lift our heads. We leave the church without a clue who accepted Jesus that day. We believe someone did, because of the 'Thank You's'

uttered by the pastor. We have no opportunity to now, or rejoice with the new saint.

One day later, or possibly a week, the new convert can slip back into the world just like they slipped their hand up for prayer, and no one will notice. There is no one to exhort them to carry on, and no one to disciple them.

I believe for the most part, it would be best to have no altar call at all, rather than create 'secret Christians.' Why not a bold declaration before God, and the saints, what we have done? One that will set our face like flint upon Him.

Pastor, as he has done in every case that I know of, heard what the Lord was speaking to him. He received it, went to the Lord with it, and changes began in our church. God is pleased with that sort of response. His exhortation, rebuke, or encouragement is for our good, and for the good of His Kingdom. We should embrace it, even beg for it. It changes everything, when we heed it.

Maureen and I have been in many churches around the world, but are most familiar with the Western Church. We can see that the three things above are not isolated to this church. This 'storefront church' is likely a cross section of the Western Church.

Let's hope that the changes made here will also be a future cross section of the Church around the world.

In closing, please remember, if we are not 'Building His Church,' we are likely tearing it down.

Chapter 15

Unshackled and Set Free

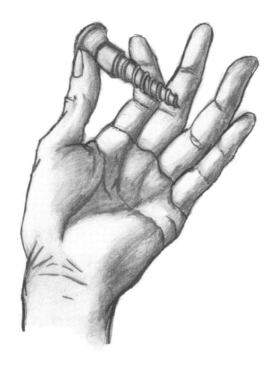

Written by: Maureen Williamson

I was twenty-two years old, and at the height of my modeling career. My eyes were set on the things of the world, and I was making great strides to fame and fortune.

Modeling had been my profession since age seven. I was encouraged into this world because of my precocious confidence, and height. My long term aim was Hollywood and I had everything going for me to achieve this dream. Photographic and Ramp

147

Modeling offers kept coming and I was choosing the most lucrative assignments.

On this fateful day, for some obscure reason, I traveled by bus into an area in Johannesburg, South Africa where I had not previously been. I was standing at a bus stop waiting for my bus. I was quite proud of my stunning, bright pink, slack suit. Suddenly, I was flung high into the air, amongst much screeching of brakes, and confusion. I came to a stop after sliding underneath a parked car and lay there covered with blood. I was scraped off the pavement and loaded into an ambulance that had arrived pronto. The seriousness of the injuries, was such that the ambulance was actually stopped by the local police for speeding in route to the hospital.

A Jewish woman, late for a dentist appointment, had approached a public transportation bus from the rear at a high rate of speed in her car, and when the bus suddenly stopped, she wasn't prepared for it. She veered her vehicle to miss the bus, and traveled onto the sidewalk striking two of us who stood there. My injuries were concentrated in my legs, and my life would never to be the same again. In a flash, my modeling career was over.

The other victim suffered greatly over the coming months, unable to feed or dress herself. She eventually died of her injuries.

In the hospital they battled to put me back together, and questioned if I would ever walk again. Both legs were broken in a total of eight places. My right ankle was all but severed. The cream of South African Orthopedic Surgeons contested with gangrene while securing what was left of my ankle with a screw more than an inch and a half in length. Skin was taken from my thigh and graphed onto my right ankle.

I was in plaster casts for two years; the first six months, in traction. The two years passed with nothing on my mind but recovery. My shattered dreams were more painful for me than the shattered bones. I was alive, but that was about all.

Finally, with my dreams far behind me, I did recover and began to work again, but never as a model. However, I found little fulfillment in life until I met Jesus Christ ten years later. At that point, I found new dreams. I set out to make a difference in the world for Him.

For thirty-four years I walked around, mostly in high heel shoes, with the ankle screw in place. I had resigned myself to living with it for life. It had been recommended that I have the screw removed after five years, but the cost seemed astronomical compared to my less than weighty budget.

It now became clear that something was seriously wrong, as my mobility became very restricted because of pain. Every step had to be calculated and counted. It felt like I was walking with stalagmites and stalactites wedged inside my right ankle. It was especially uncomfortable when in a frozen food department of any store where the cold air drops to floor level.

Few people knew of my ankle problem, or of my dream to have the screw removed. Therefore, it was a surprise when a Christian woman, a new acquaintance, telephoned, and said, "The Lord wants us to come see you."

My husband, Bill, said to them, "Well, if the Lord said to come, then come." It was two hours past our normal bedtime. She and her husband did come, and asked some questions about my ankle injury, and the cost associated with the screw removal. The woman looked at her husband and said, "The Lord asked us to pay for the surgery." At that, her husband pulled a checkbook from his pocket, and wrote a check in the amount of the surgery costs. We were flabbergasted, and praised the Lord.

After two months of anticipation, and holding tightly onto the money, surgery finally took place. The surgeon removed a number of bone spurs, some twisted scar tissue, and the ancient screw. He had wondered what sort of screw would have been used in South Africa thirty-four years ago, and thought maybe he wouldn't have the proper screw driver. His humor helped reduce the tension of the pending surgery.

In the recovery room of the lovely Parkway Surgical Clinic in Henderson, Nevada, I was handed the screw. The moment it was placed in my hand, is one never to be forgotten. Tears streamed down my cheeks, and I felt liberated from a shackle that had kept me from soaring. I was free at last.

Recalling how rebellious I had once been, a picture flooded my mind. It was as if the Lord had seen my waywardness, and saw no other solution but to do what Bible time Shepard's would do with wayward lambs.

I recently read where a Shepard, often times, would actually break the legs of a rebellious lamb who would not stay with the flock. The Shepard would then mend the legs with splints, and carry the lamb around his neck, upon his shoulders, until the legs were healed. Once the healing was complete, the lamb had no desire to leave the side of the Shepard.

It's as though He broke my legs, and then hung me around his neck for as long as it would take for my legs to heal. I came to know in time, that it was a wonderful neck, and when my legs healed, my waywardness was no more. I had learned, in pain, to trust the Shepard, and would never wander off on my own again.

All those years of carrying that screw, and now I was free. My world looked bigger and brighter, and I felt like I could now soar like an eagle. I felt like walking, leaping, and praising God, especially when the surgeon came to tell me, in my still drugged state, that the previous pain was caused by the bone spurs which had been removed.

While recuperating at home, I wondered why the couple that had blessed us with the finances for the surgery had not been in touch. I telephoned them, and immediately sensed that something was wrong. The tone of the woman's voice was different. Instead of comfort, I received words of harshness and unkindness. I was wrongly accused. It felt like a knife was being turned in my stomach, and I literally fell off the chair that I was sitting on. It transpired, that I did not come up to the expectation of what, in their mind, a missionary was. I was flabbergasted a second time.

This attack came to steal the joy of my new freedom, but I clung to what the Word of God says in Matthew 5:11-12. *"Blessed are ye, when men shall revile you, and persecute you, and shall say all manner of evil against you falsely, for my sake. Rejoice, and be exceeding glad: for great is your reward in heaven: for so persecuted they the prophets which were before you."*

Pale in the face, I shared what had transpired with my precious husband, who came in shortly thereafter. Within the hour, we returned the full amount they had given us. God was aware of all this and was not taken by surprise. In fact, God provided another financial gift that enabled us to pay the full amount of the surgery. Their gift had turned from a blessing, into a debt, and we were delighted that the Lord allowed us to step out from under the weight of it.

We resolved that nothing would rob us of our God given joy. Forgiveness flows from us and we move on. We count the cost of living our lives for Him, and know that, *"all things work together for good to them that love God, to them who are the called according to his purpose."* (Romans 8:28).

There is no place in the life of a believer in Jesus Christ for unforgiveness. We are thankful for the couple who gave, that the surgery might be scheduled. Although their actions, and words, made it impossible to keep their gift, it had prompted the surgery process to begin. And our God is faithful to finish every work He begins. We are filled with thankfulness to our God for His goodness in taking care of my ankle problem, and providing an alternate means of payment.

Indeed, I am unshackled, and set free.

Chapter 16

Middle East, Somewhere Near Kansas

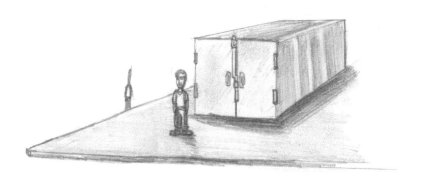

Written by: Bill Williamson

The lady approached me smiling, "where are you moving to," she asked?

"The Middle East," I said.

"Oh! Somewhere near Kansas," she replied.

She couldn't get her thinking to go abroad. Her world was America and her mind had not spent much time outside it's borders. Maureen and I loved the Middle East, particularly Israel.

The Lord had instructed Maureen and I to give up everything once again, and 'go,' this time to the Mediterranean island nation of Cyprus located in the Middle East.

Cyprus would argue that it is part of Europe rather than the Middle East, but it is located just 40 miles from Turkey, 60 miles from Lebanon and Syria, and about 100 mile from Israel. Egypt lies 200 miles to the south, and Greece to the west. Cyprus is separated from all of these nations by the beautiful waters of the Mediterranean Sea.

As a result of September 11th at the Twin Towers in Manhattan, and daily bombings and unrest in Israel, many had asked us if we were still going to the Middle East. Our answer was an easy one. 'Yes, of course, we're still going.'

Cyprus is about the size of Israel, roughly 200 miles east and west, and 50 miles north and south. In 1974 Turkey invaded the Island and took the northern one third of the island, and the Cypriots hold the remainder. Much bitterness still exists between the two sides. A United Nations buffer zone separated the two sides until recently when negotiations opened the disputed border.

The nearly empty Olympic Airways Airbus was a vivid reminder of the fear that had gripped America on September 11th. Many passengers made full length beds of adjoining empty seats for the overnight journey to Athens.

We had purchased two separate tickets, Las Vegas to Athens, and Athens to Cyprus. That meant in Athens we had to leave the Transit Passenger area in order to get our luggage and check it onto our Cyprus flight. My American passport was stamped immediately with the required Visa. But, upon presentation of Maureen's South African passport, she was flatly denied. Greece was not interested in granting South African's entry, even for retrieving luggage and passing on to Cyprus.

We had bought 'one way' tickets to Cyprus. The Greek Immigration Officer insisted that Cyprus would not let us enter without a return ticket to the USA. A phone call to Cyprus by the officer confirmed her statement.

I asked the officer to just let us go and we would take our chances in Cyprus. If they would not let us enter, we would purchase a ticket back to the states from there. We were convinced there would be no problem in Cyprus. "Why?" Because the Lord had sent us.

The officer finally agreed and let us proceed.

Larnaca International Airport was bustling with people as we moved into immigration. Cyprus, like Greece, did not favor South African travelers. An American, or European, could come for three months without charge for a Tourist Visa, my passport was quickly stamped. Maureen was offered a thirty day Tourist Visa, and was to be charged five Cypriot Pounds, about eight U.S. dollars. We explained our situation and asked that they give her three months, the same consideration as me, her husband. They refused.

Upon return to the officer's stall with the five Pounds, I found he and Maureen laughing and conversing. Everything had changed. As Maureen shared with him something about her life, praying all the while, his mind was changed. I gave him the five Pounds, he stamped her passport with the three month Visa. We left to hail a taxi, rejoicing in the goodness of the Lord.

We rented a house in a village called Lania. It was a well known village of 123 population that dated back seven hundred years. Lania was a popular stop for numerous tourist buses that toured throughout the island.

We knew right from the start that we would open our home to guests, mostly believers who were working in Israel and needed a place to come for the purpose of renewing their Tourist Visas. Also a place for them to rest and recuperate from the tensions inherent in Israel since the second intifada had begun.

We had pictured in our mind a house with many arches in the true Greek fashion. Cyprus is not part of Greece, but does have close ties. The language is Greek, the Greek flag flies at all Greek Orthodox churches, and the weather, terrain, and culture are steeped in Greek resemblances.

The house was large with fourteen arches on the veranda that adorned three sides of the house. It was complete with tile floors, six beautiful slider glass doors, orchard, and a rose garden. And all of this in a peaceful country setting near the Troodos Mountains.

We began working and improving the gardens immediately. We wanted them to be outstanding for guests that we knew would come from Israel. Christian workers in Israel were required to leave every three months for Visa renewal and we had made it known our home was open to them.

It was in anticipation of our first guests that the thought occurred to me that we could open ourselves to a variety of 'flakes' by opening our doors to just anyone who wanted to come. This concern didn't seem to go away, and I finally talked with my friend, and pastor, in Nevada. He said, "maybe God will send you some 'flakes,' just to see how you do. Just welcome them with love."

It was right there we developed our policy. We prayed, "God, don't let anyone come unless it's your will that they be here." And we determined that He would do that, and anyone who requested to come, we said, "yes, please come." We also determined that there would never be any charge to our guests, that the Lord Himself would provide all that was needed to take care of us, and them.

By now the sunny weather that had greeted us to Cyprus had faded away into a damp and colder winter scene. The leaves had withered and fallen off the grape vines, the fruit trees and roses. Snow was visible on the slopes of Mount Olympus high in the

Troodos Mountains, the highest point on the island which was visible from many of our windows.

Although beautiful, we found our house difficult to heat. We were into the hardest winter in ten years and our ceiling consisted of only thin pine boards. They were lovely to look at, but without insulation overhead, were totally inadequate to keep out the cold air that raced through the breezy attic area above.

Some of our guests would endure much discomfort. However, not one complained. Truly 'Christian' in attitude, and happy to have a roof over their head, and warm food.

One pair of guest came from the region of the Galilee in Israel. We had advised them to bring a sleeping bag or blankets. Oh how we were blessed by these two, one American, the other French. While with us fierce electric storms bombarded Cyprus, bringing thunder, rain, snow, and winds from the north that had swooped out of Russia, across eastern Europe, through Turkey, and across the cold Mediterranean. Wind speeds were reported above 100 kilometers per hour.

Mary and Josiane huddled with us around the heater in the kitchen, eating what we could prepare without electricity when the power was interrupted. By night they would read by candlelight, and during the day they would bundle up, and brave the wet, cold elements and walk the mile to Lania village.

Lania Village contained several tourist souvenir shops, a grocery market, two coffee shops, and a post office. Christos, the postman, and Andreas, who was the finance manager for the village shared the one room post office. Christos, who was in his seventies, often sat in an old wooden chair sorting mail in his lap. When we asked about a post office box to receive mail, Christos pulled a cardboard box from under a cluttered table and searched through batches of keys bound together by bailing twine. He finally found one and handed it to us.

Forty-eight guests would come to us in our fifteen month stay in Cyprus. Most of those from Israel. Circumstances were often difficult in different ways, but each was our honored guest.

The Olson's came on short notice and arrived at our Lania home after midnight from Larnaca Airport. We had no transportation. Our guest's only recourse at that time was to hire a taxi for the hour and a half ride to Lania. The cost was about $50 U.S., one way.

Maureen and I were up at 5:00 AM. The Olson's slept on, taking advantage of a well deserved break from Israel. The pressure of daily life in a country threatened by almost daily bomb blasts and suicide bombers was intense and our guests usually felt a great weight lifted as they arrived in our Cyprus home near the mountains.

There was little in the house to eat. Certainly not enough for a family of five! Our guests were not aware of the situation and we preferred they not be. We figured God would make a way. We sat across the kitchen table from one another and held hands. We prayed and the tears began to fall as we wept.

I felt God instruct me to go to the village and spend what we had; that was one and a half Cypriot Pounds. Just over two dollars. One pound, fifty was the price of tickets to town on the village bus, we tried to keep this amount on hand.

I walked the mile up to Lania and found the market open. It was open only between 6:00 and 9:00 A.M. I bought village bread, farm yard eggs, milk, and a small jar of jelly. At least we could feed the Olson's breakfast.

Seth was the oldest Olson child at seven years old. He came from the living room where he had slept on the sofa. He swung the refrigerator open, spun around and looked at us. He closed the door and ran for the bedroom saying, "Abba, ainly okel, (In Hebrew, 'father, there is no food!')"

They all eventually appeared and after being fed they inquired about going into town. We explained that a taxi was the only option, and they opted for that and we were soon on our way to Limassol. As we went out the door, Greg, pressed sixty pounds into my hand and said, "this will help with groceries." It certainly did!

Earlier that day, our dear friend, Anne, from the village of Paralimni at the east end of the island called to say that she was bringing some things for us. Anne had been a blessing to us many times in Cyprus.

Anne arrived and to our surprise she had boxes of food. She had felt from the Lord that we needed supplies, and she responded in her usual fashion. Our cupboards and refrigerator began to bulge from what she brought.

We had much need in Cyprus, especially when guests would arrive it seems, but God always made a way. And often used our guests in the process of blessing us.

On another occasion we had no food in the house, nor bus fare into town some 15 miles away. At times our one mile walk to our post box in Lania Village would result in a monetary gift and this particular day we were hopeful that would be the case.

As I walked along the winding vineyard road that climbed steeply through the terraced hillside, I talked quietly with the Lord. I told Him that our need for a gift in the mail today was great. In fact, the gift would do us no good if it were either money or check from any other country, but had to be Cypriot Pounds in order for us to pay bus fare. There was no money exchange system at Lania, nor was there any business that ever dealt in anything but Cypriot Pounds.

I remember stating that we needed a letter that contained Cypriot Pounds, and then thought, 'there is no way that can happen, who would ever have Cypriot Pounds to send.' We never received mail from within Cyprus and no one else would have the occasion to possess Pounds. I had such an expectation that some help would be in the mail box, but how would we get to Limassol, and how could we convert the money.

I climbed the final ascent into Lania, hurried between the ancient buildings on the narrow cobblestone alleyways and reached the post box. With excitement I opened the box to find an envelope with Israeli postage on it. The sender was a previous guest who had been with us. I opened the envelope to find a ten Cypriot Pound note tucked into the pages of a letter.

The explanation was that this person had carried extra Pounds home with them and had no need of it, so was sending it along to bless us. I was amazed at God's goodness, but my biggest shock came when I looked at the postmark. The letter had been sent from Israel, a mere one hundred miles away, nine weeks earlier. Letters usually came in a few days from Israel.

This letter had been delayed until this very day, a day when I would pray to God that we needed Cypriot Pounds in a letter. An awesome God had known long before that prayer that we would need Cypriot Pounds that particular day. We rejoice in a God that is so in tune with our need.

The ten Pounds, about seventeen U.S. Dollars, paid our bus fare to Limassol and provided some bare essential food items.

Zorita had come from Yugoslavia eight years earlier. She worked for a realtor and was instrumental in locating a rental house for us. Maureen and I had talked to her about Jesus and we prayed for her regularly. She shared with us her many difficulties as a single mom and also recent car troubles. Her car was an essential item in her real estate work. A recent repair expense had depleted her resources. We felt the Lord would have us do what we could to help. We asked one day if we could meet her. She agreed to meet us at the bus station.

Zorita appeared in small borrowed car. She was beaming with a wonderful smile and we greeted with hugs. She began pulling things from her car for us. Most treasured was a painting she had done of a vase with flowers especially for us. She said, "it's bright because that's what I see in you both. Bright and beautiful."

As we said our goodbyes, I pressed an envelope into her hand that contained a note and some money to help with the car repairs. We hurried to our village bus.

At home the phone rang. It was Zorita. She was crying so that it was difficult for her to talk. She managed to say these words, "now I know that Jesus is God. Only Jesus could have known what I needed." She said that now she believes in this Jesus we talk about.

Another Cypriot friend was, Andreas. Our first meeting was across the fence in front of our house. He was unloading firewood from his small pickup truck into a windrow of wood stored along the wire fence bordering our driveway.

Andreas explained that he was a retired Police Chief from Lania and was now an official of Lania Village. He owned the land where he stood and the previous year had removed the grape vineyard that had been there. Grape growing had become a liability business rather than a profitable one. He said that he would have to grow six kilos, (twelve pounds), of grapes to buy a cup of coffee.

Andreas looked at me and asked, "are you English?"

"No!" I responded, "I'm American."

He turned, walked to his pickup truck, got in and drove away.

"Wow," I thought. He must really dislike Americans. I didn't expect to talk to him again.

However, the next time we saw him, he started another conversation. We learned that Andreas was like that. When he was finished with the conversation, it was over, and he would just leave without further to do.

He came to our wall one day and said, "tomorrow I'll go wood cutting, you can go with me." I nodded, and he said, "I'll pick you up at seven."

He was there the next morning and off we went. We cut some dead Carob trees on a property that had been his father's when he was a boy. Another man, a goat farmer, now owned it. After we cut more than a pickup load the goat farmer spoke to Andreas in Greek. Andreas turned to me and said, "we will have lunch with him."

We went into the goat farmer's metal building that was quite dirty, and consisted of one large room with a full sized bed in the corner covered by a multicolored quilt. There were cluttered counter tops along two sides of the room, an old sink with water faucet, and pots and pans scattered around. There was a table with a cloth over the top that at some time in the ancient past had been white. It now had blackened stains around the edges where the dogs and goats had come to clean up the left overs.

On the table top were round loaves of Village Bread, and a plate of Halloumi cheese, (a delicious cheese made from Goat or Sheep milk). Bread crumbs from days gone by covered the table top and ants worked feverishly collecting and hauling them away. There was a jar of water from which we were each poured a glass full from. We had worked hard at wood cutting and I had been hungry, but my appetite was slipping away under my new found circumstances.

The goat farmer had a nice face, all leathery from a lifetime of sunshine. He smiled showing an uneven tooth line, and placed some homemade Halloumi on my plate. I reached for a piece of fresh sliced bread and thanked him, smiling back. The cheese was quite good and I said so. At that the farmer waved with a gesture and spoke to Andreas in Greek again saying he wanted us to take the cheese home. He dumped the remains of the plate into two used plastic bags and handed one to each of us.

Christos was another new friend. Christos and Andreas are the two most popular names on the island. This Christos ran a souvenir shop in Lania. He was well versed in English, and a bit of a philosopher, loving to analyze most anything, including religion. He had a good moral base and could quote many sayings of Jesus. We often talked of bible things, and the need to have Jesus as savior. We talked too, of where Jesus' mother, Mary, fit into the picture.

Mary was held in high esteem in Cyprus. The Greek Orthodox church believed that she was the mother of God Himself. Of course this is not true, and we tried to present this truth as often as possible. Mary is the mother of Jesus, but their concept was that as mother of God Himself, she must be above God. They literally worshiped Mary.

Aphrodite was worshiped as the 'goddess of love' in Cyprus in ancient days, and the affect can still be seen throughout the island. Pornography is found easily in the tourist shops and displayed for all to see on the busy sidewalks of tourist areas. Girls are scantily dressed in tight fitting cloths, and billboards often display tempting, lustful scenes. Nudity can be found on the beaches, but oddly enough, it's the Europeans that seem to favor pulling their bathing suit tops off. Rarely is a Cypriot seen doing so. There are beaches that are strictly Cypriot, and bare tops are rarely seen on them.

It was odd that 'Lust' and 'Religion' were the two obvious spiritual forces on the island.

One day in Christos' shop we found a new array of calendars displaying nude women. I found opportunity to speak with Christos and after a moment or so, I mentioned the calendars, saying that they were not honoring to God. That the female body was beautiful, but God did not create it to be displayed for men to lust over. My words seemed to come as such a surprise to him. He didn't agree, or disagree. He simply listened. Many months later we would leave Cyprus and the calendars were still displayed.

After a few winter months in Cyprus spring arrived with a burst of leaves, blossoms, and flowers, not only in our garden, but in the countryside too.

My love for hiking the hills had not been exercised in many months and with spring in the air, I was ready. Maureen had gone with Anne in her little van to do some sight seeing. I had gone with them on many occasions, but today I would hike.

My goal was to reach the river in the valley below. Vineyard roads joined one after another and I was making my way toward the river. The roads were getting narrower and the wheel tracks were getting lost in the abundant chest high grass. Soon there was only the outline of the ancient road, the wheel tracks were gone.

I sensed I should watch for snakes. I am not afraid of snakes and have encountered many rattlesnakes in my lifetime and they are about as hazardous as they come. But, I didn't like being surprised by even the most docile of snakes. I don't know anybody that does.

Although I could see the river below me, I was still some distance from it. I peered through the grasses and took cautious steps. Suddenly, I saw something laying in the sunlight ahead of me. I stopped. I could see just a portion of a snake, a large snake. It was black and as big around as a coke bottle. I could see about three feet of it's length, but from the diameter of that portion I knew it was much longer.

I crept cautiously backward until I could climb to the top of a bank overlooking the snake. There it was! It must have been eight feet long. I looked to see if there was anything laying around that I could defend myself with, I found nothing. I looked back toward the snake; it was gone. Where, I didn't know. I decided that my effort to get to the river for that day was over.

Subsequent discussions with villagers made us aware that this was considered a 'good snake' because it ate rodents, and other snakes. However, I just didn't like the size of it. There were several poisonous snakes in Cyprus, but none were black.

We invited Andreas over for coffee in the shade of our Loquat tree one day. I asked Andreas about the snake I saw near the river. He stated very boldly and with absolute authority, "the black snake is good. The black snake is not a snake at all."

I was surprised by that statement and asked him to explain. He said, "the black snake is the one that was in the garden of Eden. It is a good snake. It's not a snake at all." As we pushed on with this thought, Andreas had no more to add to this folklore theory. We thought it odd that anyone would consider the 'serpent' of the Garden Of Eden good.

The black snake surely is a snake, and isn't necessarily so 'good.'

Maureen and I learned this one day as we strolled hand in hand along our drive way. There was a small garbage can house built into our front wall. It was large enough for two cans.

With a frightening hiss a large snake came racing at us from the garbage house. It was about seven foot in length and had raised half it's body in the air. It was black and it's mouth was open to the maximum. It came at us so fast that it was hardly possible to avoid it. Maureen turned and ran back to the gate, unlatched it and was inside in a flash. I was still trying to run backwards. I didn't want to take my eye off it. I had learned with rattlesnakes that once you take your eye off of it, it can disappear and then what do you do? How can you relax if you don't know where it went?

I soon determined that I could not run backwards fast enough. But, suddenly the snake dropped its full length to the ground and turned away. It slithered across the dirt driveway and tried to go through the green mesh material on the fence. Unable to find a way it became irritated and began smashing against the mesh again and again. Finally it turned further away from us and went around the end of the fence and disappeared into Andreas' wood pile.

That ended our walk for that day. So much for black snakes being harmless. It was good to see that Maureen's less than 100% ankle kept her in good stead during the attack, and retreat.

Andreas' explanation later was that the snake must have had eggs, or young snakes, in the wood pile. We were to see many black snakes after that, but none quite like this one. We're still not convinced that a 'black snake' is a 'good snake.'

Our guests generally came to stay four days, but some would request longer stays. Kerry was one who did. Kerry, a young American, had been in Israel quite some time and needed a place to come pray, and seek the Lord. Kerry came longing for direction from the Lord for his future and he would not be deterred from doing just that. He was diligent to spend time in prayer and reading the Word.

Kerry sometimes worked in our garden, cleaned our veranda and did other things to be helpful. Kerry was quiet, and often we would not see him throughout the day. Although we prepared three meals a day for our guests, he would sometimes fast and not require meals. He was always pleasant and courteous.

It was Kerry's last evening meal with us. We sat on the veranda and Kerry chose to pray for the meal. In the prayer he spoke words similar to these: "Lord, bless Bill and Maureen. When I was hungry they fed me, when I had no place to stay, they gave me a bed." He went on, but these words were etched in our minds and hearts at that moment, and they remain today.

There were times when we would get weary of hosting guests, wanting only to rest ourselves. But, we remembered Kerry's prayer and were motivated to serve yet another guest. Each guest was a blessing in one way or another.

Cyprus is considered, 'Christian.' We were delighted to hear that when we began making plans to go. But, we found many are 'Christian' in word only. We found few Greek Cypriots with a relationship with Jesus. Most have a relationship with the 'Church,' or the 'Priest.' We found, at least some, priests were heavy drinkers, and walked the streets as one to be highly honored. I watched one elderly lady give her seat to a priest at the bus station, all the while kissing his hands. The priest took the seat and seemed to be enjoying this adoration.

Our born again pastor, Miltos, tells us that many Greek Orthodox priests don't actually believe in God. They are atheist. They seek after the priestly position because it is a 'good job,' with power and lots of 'benefits.'

Every village had a Greek Orthodox Church, and we would hear the bells tolling from the three villages near our house. The church in our village of Lania displays a statue of the Virgin Mary at the entrance.

Icons of Mary, Jesus, and Saints adorn the walls and mantles of the Cypriot home, business offices, and nearly every vehicle has multiple icons present. The icons are highly esteemed as well. We found these religious icons sold on one side of the shop isle, while pornography was sold on the other side. Jesus, when displayed, would appear crucified on a cross, or still a baby in his mother's arms. The icons often displayed a mourning mother with her bloody crucified son in her arms. This is a Jesus with no power. A Jesus that had not had victory. Prayers were often made to this pitiful Mary, rather than God, or Jesus.

The true believer of God and His resurrected Son, were few in Cyprus. I mean one who has been born again, by asking forgiveness, repenting of sins, and choosing to follow Jesus. One source informed us that there were two thousand born again believers on the island. Our Cypriot pastor felt there were closer to five hundred. This is an island with 700,000 people. Wow! That's a poor percentage, less than one tenth of one percent. Even the most radical Moslem country has a higher percentage.

Churches, as we in the West understand the church, are few. We learned of only five in Limassol, (a city of more than 200,000 people), during our time there. We preferred to have a Cypriot pastor in a church where the congregation was largely Cypriot, we found only two, and just one to our liking.

Pastor Miltos and his wife, Paula, had led this church for nearly twenty seven years. They were sound in their walk of faith, and tried to pattern the church after the New Testament model. Miltos freely gave up his pulpit so that others of the congregation could bring a word, and many were able to stand and share a word from the Lord.

The preaching and teaching was done in Greek and translated into English. It was also translated into the Sri Lankan language as there were a good number of Sri Lankans present. Song books were provided in both Greek and English. Maureen and I used English, but the worship team led in Greek. Sometimes it was difficult to sing along. We learned at the close of one song, that we had been on the wrong page the whole time. But, we had followed along making the words fit the music.

We discovered the makeshift village bus system after a few weeks. The bus was always filled with interested characters, some carried produce to sell at the open market. Most though, were traveling to the hospital, utility offices, or city center for shopping.

We were surprised one day returning from Limassol when the bus driver missed his turn off to Lania from the Troodos Highway. The passengers let out a roar as if on cue, they were sure they had caught him in a terrible mistake. But, he simply looked in his large rear view mirror and yelled a response in Greek. At that, they all turned and looked at us causing us to wonder what he had said, and how we fit into it.

Another half mile along Troodos Highway he pulled into the side road that led to our house. He made a large swing, stopped, opened the entrance door, looked at us, and spoke. We jumped from our seats, grabbed our heavy grocery bags and headed for the door. We looked back at him and spoke a greeting of thanks. He beamed and closed the door, swung the bus around and headed back to the Lania Village road.

He had saved us a mile walk along the rough vineyard road. Apparently he had learned from one of the villagers where we actually lived, and thereafter he always dropped us off at our road.

We found other friends in the bus station area of Limassol. One older man who sold goods from a container at the bus station was one such person.

Maureen and I stood at the street corner near his container one morning waiting for Yianna, our landlady. The old man came across the street carrying an armload of supplies for his business. He sat them down and attempted to open the container doors. This

169

container was of the type used to haul goods aboard ships overseas. It had large full height doors that met in the middle of the end of the container. A handle moved a long rusty rod that protruded into slots at the top and bottom of the container.

He struggled unsuccessfully to move the lever. I stepped to the container offering my help and was able to open it quickly. He was grateful and we were fast friends from that point on. The door was a constant problem for him and I helped him again on another occasion.

One day while shopping we spied some WD-40, and it occurred to me that this was just what the old man needed for his container doors. We purchased the can, and proceeded to the bus station. I presented it to him pointing at the rusty rod and hinges, indicating what it was for. He held it up to the neighboring merchant to see. He was happy for the gift, and that ended his struggle with the doors.

We began speaking to him at every encounter. This man spoke a few words of English. Not well, but enough to express himself. His English was much better than our Greek.

One day I got off the village bus and saw him wearing black trousers and shirt. His head was hanging and he was moving slowly without the usual enthusiasm. He sat there in a mournful state. I approached and asked if he was OK. He raised both hands, and his eyes, to heaven, tears slipping from his eyes, "my wife," he said. I touched his shoulder and expressed my sympathies as best I could. I listened as he explained she was his wife of sixty years, how they had survived the invasion in the north and come to Limassol twenty six years ago, and how he couldn't understand why God would take her.

I felt such a loss of words at this important moment. This man needed comfort and I could give him little because of the language barrier.

I explained to Maureen when I got home. We purposed to spend at least a few minutes with him when we came into town. Each time we got off the bus we would look for him. Maureen was so good to put her arm around his shoulder, or squeeze his hand. We would listen as he spoke. His eyes and hands always went toward heaven with a questioning tone in his voice.

Another time, I sat with him and he had little to say. I sat there on the curb for the longest time. We watched the people go by, the cars and buses go by, and no words came. Soon it was time for my bus, I took his hand, squeezed it and said a farewell.

For two months this went on, he wore the same black trousers and shirt, and it was plain to see that he was not adjusting to the loss of his wife so well.

We shared what we knew of this man with Pastor Miltos, asking if he would come with us to meet the man. We knew Miltos could communicate the love of Jesus to him. We drove into the city center hoping he was there. He was! The man's face lit up as he saw us approach. I introduced him to our friends, Miltos and Paula.

Miltos talked briefly with him, but one thing the man said will be etched forever in our memory. Miltos told him that I was a 'godly man.' At that the old man looked at me and Maureen, and said, "I'll believe anything they tell me."

That scared me at first, but then saw what power love has. We had simply loved this man, and had made an effort to extend compassion and care to him. God had touched his heart and he was willing, not only to listen, but to believe.

The old man nodded continually in agreement as Miltos shared about Jesus. Maureen and I were able to speak, but had little to say that Miltos hadn't covered wonderfully. Miltos came to see him other times, bringing him reading material, and encouraging him to seek and pray to God believing in Jesus Christ.

The last time we saw him he gave us a pair of satin embroidered pillow slips as a token of his friendship. We remember this man often and pray that he is growing in Christ and recovering from his grief.

We had been without transportation for ten months. We rode village buses, sometimes gleaned a few hours of rental car use, and had literally walked hundreds of miles. Walking the two miles round trip to Lania Village from our house daily for mail and groceries for that ten months would amount to 480 miles. Of course there were days when that walk wasn't made, but there were days when it was done twice.

Maureen's ankle hindered her walking, especially over the eroded and rocky vineyard road with it's steep inclines leading up to Lania Village. But she did make that walk many times. Once it was done while a blanket of snow lay across the landscape. Maureen often spent weeks in our Lania home without getting into town. We had prayed constantly for ten months for a car. Through a wonderful gift from our Nevada church, a little blue Peugeot sedan was soon to be ours. We named it 'blessing,' a name more missionaries likely use for their cars than any other.

Rumors of war were in the air. The US had given Iraq ultimatums and would attack if Saddam would not comply.

Since September 11th, 2001, Americans had been trained by circumstances to suspect, even be fearful or suspicious of Arabs, especially those from the Middle East. Any American could fear being knifed while walking through an alley in any Middle East country. While we did not make that a life concern that would trouble us each day, one could not erase thoughts completely when encountering someone who fit the September 11th profile.

Amir fit that profile. In his forties, dark skinned, dark hair with streaks of grey, a trimmed beard framing his broad chin, and he was Moslem.

Amir was from Iran. He made it clear though that he was not Arab, but Persian. He had a friend, Ishmael. They had both come to Cyprus from Iran some years earlier to work. Work was scarce in Iran and both sent money home to families. Amir had a particularly hard story. Because of his disdain for the way Iran was run by the ruling Islamic party, he was vocal about it. His vocal attitude landed him in prison for three years. His hope was that change would occur in Iran. He felt that he could not go back until the regime had changed.

We met Amir and Ishmael on Christmas day in a friend's Lania home. In her usual fashion, Maureen attached herself to them in an effort to have them know Jesus Christ, and His gospel. We planned to meet another time and eventually arranged to take the two of them to another village to a believer's home for dinner.

We picked them up near their apartment in Limassol. They hopped into the back seat of the Peugeot and we sped away into the darkness. We drove east toward the village of Pyrgos. As we traveled through the darkness, Amir's profile began to be the subject of my thoughts. He was sitting directly behind me and I thought about how perfect this would be if he and his friend were Moslems who hated Americans. I began to imagine 'cold steel' being placed against the back of my neck, or along the front of my throat.

These thoughts soon melted away as they laughed and shared more about their lives. These were two men who liked Americans, hated injustice, and wanted change in their homeland of Iran. They were open to meet, socialize and share thoughts with born again believers. Any hint of fear vanished.

We had a good evening with them. They joined hands with us around the dinner table while we prayed over our meal in Jesus' name.

A week later we were invited to Amir's for a meal. The apartment had scant furnishings and the walls were bare except two

173

banners written in Arabic. Ishmael prepared most of the traditional Iranian meal. It was tasteful and plentiful, and we learned to eat with a fork and spoon, the Iranian way, rather than a knife and fork.

At one point, Amir was sitting on one side of the dinner table and we on the other. It appeared as if he could have been interviewing us. Ishmael had begun filming us with his camcorder. Amir with the Arabic banner just over his head, looked like someone from many of the scenes we had seen in Al Quaida tapes. I commented on this and he picked up on that line and began discussing, in fun, payment of information from us. We joined in and constructed a story line that could have seemed a conspiracy.

The thought then occurred to me, here we are being filmed in what could appear to be a real situation. Concern returned once again. I began to play down the scene and we moved on to other discussion. We had a great laugh over the skit, but thoughts lingered for weeks about that film footage. Again, unfounded fear.

Just back from a visit across the Mediterranean in Israel, our first trip to our Lania Post Office box yielded an envelope from the United States State Department. Inside was a fist full of papers stating it was time for Maureen's immigration interview at the American Embassy. Her application for permanent residence in the USA was about to be approved.

We began praying, "where to, Lord?" We knew we must return to the states, but where? I had no preconceived idea, I just wanted to be where the Lord wanted to send us.

It was in Maureen's heart to go to Florida. I told her Florida would be fine if the Lord wanted that. I purposed over the following days to bring that specifically to the Lord in my morning quiet times and ask the question, "what's this about Florida, Lord?"

His answer was sudden and surprising to me, "that's where I want you to go."

I said, "yes, Lord." Florida suddenly became our destination, and I looked forward to it. I knew that if the Lord wanted us in Florida that no other place would do. But where in Florida? We had never lived in Florida. Both of us had visited, but knew nothing except it had lots of palm trees, and pretty beaches.

Soon after we knew it was Florida, a guest arrived from Israel. Aviah had come from Jerusalem for much needed break. She came through the swinging doors at Larnaca International Airport, strode over to us beaming with a great smile and said, "I bring you greetings from Hezi and Davida in Arcadia, Florida. Maureen had met Hezi and Davida years earlier in Israel. Aviah had been on the phone with them the previous evening.

Although we had never heard the name, Arcadia, something was pricked in my heart. I kept it to myself. Early the next morning, I spent time with the Lord for prayer, listening, and reading of His Word. I asked about Arcadia. His answer was like the Florida answer, quick and short, "that's where I want you to go." Several days of prayer settled it, Arcadia it would be.

Our pastor and good friend from Boulder City, Nevada made a whirlwind trip to Cyprus. He and his wife had flown to Germany to spend Christmas with family. Only four hours by air from Cyprus, he didn't want to miss a chance to see two of their missionaries. We felt very much a part of the Boulder City church, and welcomed his visit.

A whirlwind it was. He arrived in Paphos at the west end of the island, spent one night in our home, and flew out of Larnaca at the east end of the island thirty-six hours later. But, in-between we were able to see a lot of Cyprus. In Nicosia, we drove up the boulevard toward the American Embassy. When the American flag came into view the three of us burst into song, "Oh say can you see, by the dawn's early light......" The American anthem rang off our lips. It was spontaneous because our hearts were truly stirred at the sight of our American flag.

Our greatest surprise was when Maureen, a South African, joined right in with Duane and I as if she had sang it all her life. She, perhaps, had more reason to sing, she was to be sworn in at this Embassy in a few days.

Days later, and it was time for the interview at the Embassy. We arrived early on a wet December day. The door was locked and we stood in a light rain until 8:30 AM. We were told to expect up to four hours of interview. Soon we stood before the American Consulate who had Maureen's packet, that was quite heavy from two years of paperwork, in front of him.

He said, "raise your right hand," looking at Maureen. She did and the swearing in ceremony began. It was short, but memorable. There was little interview. We had expected many questions, but we were out of the building in forty-five minutes. We returned in two hours for the completed paperwork.

Little was left of our Cyprus experience. We had come in obedience to our Lord, Jesus. We would now go in obedience to Him.

We flew away in the darkness of early morning, and there would be little view of Cyprus below us. Cyprus had certainly changed us, we wondered if there would be any changes in Cyprus because we came. We hoped and prayed so.

We were in and out of London in a flash and soon America bound.

Orlando International Airport was much larger that we thought. But, Immigration was relaxed and informal. Maureen's papers were quickly processed and she was handed her Permanent Resident stamped passport. Her Green Card would follow in the mail. Soon we were outside searching for a rental car to take us to Arcadia.

We were ready for an American adventure!

Chapter 17

Little Town of Arcadia

Written by: Maureen Williamson

The life of a believer requires hearing and obeying the Lord. But once you've heard and obeyed there are often questions such as this one that arose in the little town of Arcadia, 'what is our purpose for being here, Lord?'

God told us to move to Arcadia, Florida. Did we know anything about Arcadia? No, we didn't even know which airport to fly to. We came out of sheer obedience and blind to what awaited us.

I had a dreamy idea of Florida with swaying palm trees, white sand beaches and endless sunshine. This fabulous picture was not what I found Arcadia to be. Arcadia is rural America, cattle and orange country. Basically, a depressed area where not much happens. A time capsule of Arcadia would contain cowboys, saloons, hangings, rodeos, migrant workers, racoons, armadillos, alligators, and fabulous migrating birds. No decent shops, but beautiful oak trees and draping Tarzan type vines everywhere. 'What is our purpose for being here,' I wondered?

The Lord had told us that He was going to establish us in a home of our own. And without a means of a down payment, by faith, we started the process of looking for a suitable house to buy. This began a new experience for Bill and I, having only dreamed of a home of our own in the past.

We rented a small furnished mobile home with no air conditioning. We often used the refrigerator freezer to cool our heads in temperatures that soared into the 90's that spring. Our search went on for the kind of house we could enjoy; a place suitable for our many guests; a place of peace and serenity.

When we had exhausted all avenues to find something that we liked the Lord led us to a secluded house that we immediately knew was for us. An ideal setting hidden away with orange groves in one direction, a pasture with cows in another direction, and in yet another view, a beautiful white horse pranced energetically along the fence line. The rest, and best views of all, dozens of acres of mown grass, almost luminous green, everywhere we looked.

The house was finally ours and eighteen months of back breaking hard labor began, and again I thought, 'what is our purpose for being here?' It was nothing but work, work, and more work.

Exceedingly hard times were part of this period and our faith was seriously tested. Our worst day we both remember so vividly was preparing and eating the last food in our house, some awful fried bread made with only water and flour that had ants in it. Our financial support just dried up when we returned to America and we marveled at how this could happen, we are the same two people with the same vision and yet the money simply was not there.

In and through it all, deep down we knew this was a test; God always has His reasons and purposes for allowing such times to come into the lives of his children. Godly character is what is being built internally in difficult times.

We purposed not to tell anyone, other than God himself, that we were in such need, but that morning I remember saying to the Lord that if somebody, anybody, spoke to us at Church, where we were headed with an empty petrol tank, I would say something about our lack.

As we walked into the car park after church, curious if the fumes in our petrol tank would get us home, I had tears in my eyes, wondering again, 'what is our purpose for being here?'

A man from the church spoke behind us and approached with an invitation to come have lunch with them. We had no idea if we were to pay, or what. I broke down and said, 'we don't have money for lunch and not even enough petrol to get us home.' The man immediately handed us money and said to follow him and his wife to the petrol station. They then took us to lunch, and also provided us with all kinds of foodstuffs that same evening. They gave with a smile of love from their hearts. That event was a major turning point for us.

We pressed on being involved in a street ministry feeding the people and got involved in other Church activities reaching the lost. We were approached and agreed to do the Church monthly newsletter as a gift to the local body of Christ, which we still do to this day. We witnessed for the Lord as we always do, after all witnessing is not a location thing, it's a lifestyle.

181

Nearing completion of the house remodeling, the Lord told Bill that when the last floor tile was laid that he had a job for him at the local Home Building Supply store. Here comes another huge adjustment for me, stuck out in the middle of nowhere alone without my beloved for eight hours a day. With little money and the added chores that Bill normally did but no longer had time for, more than ever I was wondering, 'what is our purpose for being here?'

I wasn't a happy camper. I longed for Israel, for places to go and people to meet, and wondered what had happened to my once exciting life. It was hard trying to get to know the local people who clearly found me to be foreign, and for once in my life that was not an advantage. Everybody noticed my accent but when they would enquire where I was from I could see in their eyes that exotic places like Zimbabwe, South Africa, Israel, and Cyprus just did not register. 'Ooi va vooi,' as they say in Hebrew, (oh, dear me). I was in deep weeds and I could do nothing about it.

Then one Friday morning we heard Hurricane Charley, a category 4 hurricane, that was traveling towards Tampa had changed course and was headed directly to Arcadia and would be upon us in hours. Bill and I actually encountered an element of thrill, after all we have been around and had experienced a lot of different things, but not a hurricane. Clearly we did not know what was about to happen as we watched a tornado throwing objects in the air from our back window.

The excitement was quickly wiped away as hurricane Charley hit us full force. Winds of 145 miles an hour, and the dreaded "freight train" sound that comes with a category 4 hurricane, embraced our newly remodeled home. We watched parts of our costly water system fly through the skies, and as our roof peeled off, glass and other objects from the neighborhood hit our house with a force unexplainable. The most frightening ordeal of my life went on for three hours in broad daylight.

When it was over, Bill and I foolishly took a drive into Arcadia where sparking electrical lines, downed trees and building debris were strewn everywhere. We were speechless in shock over the devastation we saw. Of all the homes around us ours was one of the least damaged but still suffered more than $26,000 loss.

Imagine; no electricity, no water, (which means no toilet use, dishes, showers, or cooking). Our baths consisted of standing under the eves of the house during the frequent rain storms that followed. Rain water was gathered in buckets for later use in the bathtub and toilet.

The phone service lasted through the hurricane but failed the next day and was not re-established for two weeks. Even cell phones were disabled due to fallen signal towers. Curfews were in place from 8 PM until 6 AM each day. No restaurants or grocery stores were open. Gas was not available for days, and then only in limited supply after enduring long lines.

Air conditioning was unavailable and temperatures soared into the upper nineties. Sleep was difficult in the heat and only periods of laying on the cooler tile floors made it possibly. Mosquitoes multiplied at a fierce rate with the innundation of rain and was only curbed by constant aerial spraying. The drone of low flying aircraft and gasoline generators could be heard throughout the long night periods.

I was taken away with a severe migraine by a family of believers to Vero Beach. Two weeks later I returned only to hear that Hurricane Frances was headed our way.

Packing in a hurry with evacuation orders I was flown to Arizona to my precious caring friend Mary, whilst Bill remained without any facilities in Arcadia, committed to his job. He would work by day at the Building Supply Store, and by evening at home doing temporary repairs to hurricane damage. Don't you think I was thinking again,'"what is our purpose for being in Florida?'

183

I returned a week later only to learn that Hurricane Jeanne would blast Arcadia in a few days. Jeanne came with a fury and ripped the wood strips loose that held the temporary roofing on our home, and pried our screened Florida Room from the side of the house and battered it relentlessly. Rain found its way in through missing soffits and poured down the wall of our newly remodeled guest room. The new carpet was soaked and only tedious effort to raise and dry the carpet saved it.

After 'Hurricane Charley,' Bill, as always, had stepped up to the plate. Armed with a flash light and words of love and comfort, he helped people who came staggering into the store where he worked; at least one bleeding and barefoot, and most all in shock over the on-going hurricanes. Into darkness of the badly damaged store the people came hoping to find something, anything, to repair their smashed homes and shattered hopes, and to keep the next hurricane out.

Christ's light of the Gospel was beaming through my husband, and suddenly I knew that Arcadia was hand picked by God for us; these hurricanes were one purpose for us being here. Instead of us being on an overseas mission field, the fact that the mission field always surrounds the believer became very clear to us.

Thinking of the hurricanes as being the worst experience of our lives God has proven to us yet again that *'All things do work together for good to those who love the Lord and are called according to His purposes.'* We have come out of it smiling, and smelling like roses. Stronger, not weaker, for the experience.

Bill and I had remodeled the interior of our home, and now God used the hurricanes and our home owner's insurance to see that the exterior was remodeled as well. The roof had needed replacement and the house was due for repainting; both before the hurricanes.

We stand in awe of what God has accomplished on our behalf and know that this is just the beginning. What the enemy meant for harm God has reversed and with the result our little piece of paradise is more beautiful than ever. He is not a man that he should lie, He said that He would establish us in a home and that is exactly what has happened.

Shortly after the hurricanes God clearly told Bill that his job was over, that His purpose had been achieved. Nobody was happier, and remains happiest, than me to have my beloved back home, a free man again. Hallelujah! We continued restoring our home and repaired all the damage.

We hold lightly all that we have though, standing ready to go and be of service wherever our Lord may choose next. The adventure goes on.

Chapter 18

Live Your Own Adventure

Written by: Bill Williamson

The previous chapters contain stories that center upon obedience. Obedience to do what our Lord commands us to do. It doesn't take a command for that matter. We only need a 'still, small voice,' to prompt us to action, whether to a down and outer sitting in the gutter, the rich and famous, or the President of Israel. It's all the same, just obey. Maureen and I press each other on to greater heights in service and obedience to our God, all the while cherishing the adventure that comes from each episode of our Christian walk. Some call this lifestyle of leaving everything behind and going in obedience to some far off land, or just going to our eighty-three neighbors, amazing.

Isn't it sad that in today's world it is considered 'amazing' to do what we as Christians are commanded to do, and should long to do?

As Christians, we are to be 'radical.' Radical in the eyes of the world. I prayed for a year and a half for opportunities to be 'radically obedient.' It is only in the past couple of years that I have realized that to God there is no such thing as 'radical' obedience. He simply sees obedience, or disobedience.

We have but one decision to make about obedience. Make it now, and pray like this.

"Lord, I decide right now to always obey your commands, however I like or dislike them."

Once we make that decision, we need never make it again. When we hear His voice we simply say, "Yes, Lord."

We say, "No, Lord," each time we refuse to respond to any request He makes of us. Saying, "No, Lord," will cause us to lose our fervor. That desire to be used by our Lord, will fade away. However, as we say, "Yes, Lord," that fervor just grows and grows, to where it is only natural to respond in this way.

You've read our stories where lives had opportunity for change because someone cared, and obeyed. But, Maureen writes in her first book, 'Audacity To Love,' on two occasions, with a drunk woman on the beach, and a crippled beggar, where she admits missing that, 'still, small voice.' And if not totally missing it, not responding to it rightly.

Even in our zeal for obeying our Lord, we miss the mark at times. But, like Maureen, who made a decision at each of those two points in her life, we can assess what had been done, and vow to grow in that area, pressing into Him deeper, lest it happen again. We will occasionally fail to hear rightly, or to obey completely. We need not beat ourselves up when we do. We simply ask for Father's help to improve our hearing, and our doing.

Are you willing to be 'radical' for Jesus?

You might say, "I don't know if I am willing."

Then, I ask, "Are you willing to be made willing?" Can you ask Father to do at least that. Once you are willing, it becomes much easier to obey. Ask Him to make you willing.

I am always encouraged to read other's episodes of obedience. They encourage and spur me on to greater heights in my own obedience to my precious Jesus. But, I have to be careful not to live my life through them. I can get caught up listening to wonderful tapes of others, reading books about others, and marveling at the amazing way God uses them. I can spend untold hours talking about someone else's adventures for Christ.

Father longs to use you and I in fabulous ways. Wouldn't you like to 'Live Your Own Adventure?' It's not always for the other person. Stop your busyness for a few moments, go to your room, your prayer closet, wherever you can get to. Fall to your knees. Pray like this.

"Father, I'm not satisfied! I'm not satisfied! No, I'm not satisfied! I want more from my life, Lord. Help me to live my own adventure. Give me a desire to live a life of obedience."

We can get lost in a sea of circumstances if our eyes are taken off Jesus for just a moment. You may have been in that predicament when you began reading this book. Start now! Slow down, listen to Father, then simply obey. Put feet to the enthusiasm gained from this book. Don't hesitate, do it now. Step out...'Live Your Own Adventure.'

Some of you are no doubt saying, "I would.... kind of like to...but I'm not really willing to risk it. Risk being changed. Risk giving up what I have."

OK, but are you willing to be 'made willing' to risk it? Pray this.

"Lord, I don't have the courage, please make me willing. I want to begin a life of obedience, and adventure. My own adventure, not through movies, books, or television. When I talk about exciting events, stories, let them be from my life. From encounters with people you set in my path, Lord."

Father God would have that all of us be living chapters of an adventure book. The adventure begins when I say, "Yes, Lord!"

Do you remember in Chapter seven of this book, how Genevieve made the most important decision of her life? She accepted Jesus as her Savior, and Lord. But she subsequently did more than that. She and Maureen became fast friends. They spent much time together at church and socially. Genevieve had a hunger to follow after her Lord, and to become like Him.

Genevieve and Maureen grew closer over the next year. Soon, Maureen knew Father God was calling her back to Israel once again. When she did near departure, Genevieve would have it no other way but to go with her. She left all that she knew of security, her job, car, and her belongings, and boarded Israel's El Al Airlines with Maureen.

Genevieve lived in Jerusalem for more than a year by faith. She saw God provide every need she had. She lacked for nothing of the essentials of life. She grew spiritually at a rapid rate, clinging to the wonderful teaching of the Word found throughout the Church in Jerusalem.

God spoke to Genevieve about moving on to another assignment. Only this time it would be on her own, without her mentor. By now Genevieve had made many new friends in Israel. It would be hard to leave them behind, but she knew she must.

Genevieve flew from Israel to London, her new location. She knew in her heart this was where she was to go. No one met her at the airport. She had no friends, no place to go, no place of security to run to. She found London large, wet and lonely. But she pursued God's purpose for her. Times grew difficult, but her determination to follow Jesus held strong.

Genevieve's living arrangements varied and were never dependable. One night, as she waited for Father's hand of provision, it became apparent there was to be no bed or room for her. She spent the night on a bench in a popular park, as drizzle came down throughout the cold night. Not a place where young ladies were advised to hang out.

Hard stuff? Yes, but Genevieve had said, "Yes, Lord." For better or for worse, she meant it. Genevieve endured London, and eventually found herself back in South Africa. She has not lost her fervor for the Lord, and has no intention of ever turning back to the old lifestyle she left behind several years ago. She knows that a wonderful future is beckoning her day by day, and she is moving in that direction, her destiny.

In an adventure of my own, during one twenty-four hour period Father ask me to do three things that could have seemed hard to someone not accustomed to saying, 'Yes, Lord!'

Early one morning I sat quietly before God. He asked me to give my car to Missionary friends several states away. I had heard of their need for dependable transportation traveling between

Montana and Canada. I said, "Yes, Lord," even though I had great need for the car. I simply trusted that he had another way for me to get about, and that some great purpose would be served as I simply obeyed Him in this way.

At mid morning that same day, I learned that the local City Council had no one to pray for the opening of their meeting. The council had begun doing this, not because they were Godly men, but because I believe God laid it on their hearts. I answered the phone when the City Clerk called to talk to my Pastor and found he was out of town. My heart broke when she told me that no one could come pray, but a prayer was being faxed in and would be read at the meeting. *(Possibly by a non-believer.)*

After hearing this, and hanging up the phone, my heart began a signal dance, the rhythm it takes on when I know Father is wanting something of me. I sensed in the Spirit that I must call the City Clerk back. I dialed and spoke to her, "I'm not a Pastor, but a Missionary. I am willing to come pray."

She was excited that she had a volunteer, and confirmed the time and place. I did open the City Council meeting with prayer that night, and Father gave me just the right words, fitting for the occasion. I had peace, even in the face of the TV cameras and a full Council Chamber that night.

Near noon of the same day, I became nearly overwhelmed with fatigue. I didn't know the cause. It was highly unusual for me. I could think of nothing but going home and laying down for a short rest. I closed the church where I was helping with remodeling, and went home. As I rested in a comfortable chair, I picked up my Bible and a piece of paper fell out. On it were three names that I had placed there to remind me to pray for their salvation.

The first name was that of my son-in-law, Aaron. I began to pray for him, and the Spirit of God began to draw me into deep intercession for his life. I began to cry out, "Save him, Lord, save him." I felt as though Father had placed His finger inside my chest. I agonized for Aaron's life.

Soon, I felt it was finished. I then sent an e mail to Aaron, explaining what God had done.

Are these three things hard? Maybe. But, when I see them as opportunities to simply be obedient, it's not so hard. I await the wondrous outcome of each of these three opportunities for 'radical' obedience.

Read our adventures, but be spurred on to 'Live Your Own.' God is no respecter of persons. What He has done for us, He will do for you.

As you've read, Maureen and I married in Bethlehem. Not long after that I had the opportunity to meet, Shlomie, of Chapter one.

Shlomie is now fifteen years older than chapter one relates. He is a nice young Jewish man. He is polite, considerate, and handsome. However, he still has not made a choice for Jesus in his life. He states he wants a religious Jewish life, and that does not include Jesus. Shlomie knows the truth, he has heard it many times from Maureen. He still listens intently, but cannot accept, nor commit to Jesus. He cannot say, "Yes, Lord," in that regard.

Accepting Jesus in Israel is not without risk for the Jew. Statistics show that no more than 4% of Israelis believe in Jesus. The remainder are adamantly against the idea. Many are radically against it, and persecute those who choose to believe. Maureen and I have seen it first hand on the streets of Jerusalem. Because Shlomie cannot see the benefit, for him, the risk outweighs any benefit.

Maureen and I pray for Shlomie, that his adventure will soon begin. We pray that Genevieve will continue in her radical obedience to our Lord. We pray for you the reader also, that you begin today to say, "Yes, Lord," to the adventure that awaits. Taste one and see that it is good.....

The city where we once lived was located on a highway where four million vehicles a year passed by our small church. They are either going to, or leaving from Las Vegas. Some call it the Gambling Capital of the world. Most are willing to take risk with their money, and most leave it behind.

There is no risk in saying 'yes' to Jesus. No way to lose. It's a 'win-win' situation. We are risk takers, why not for Jesus?

Scripture is filled with promises. We often dwell upon them to make us feel better, or to give us hope. We see the benefit of the promises, but we seldom pause to look at the cost. When we see a good deal in the physical, we most generally ask, "Yeah, but what's the bottom line?" And then we find out it cost something. And then we say, "That's what I thought."

Our promises from Father are the same way. Examine them, everyone of them has a bottom line. Something is required. Most often the cost is obedience. Test this and see for yourself. Go to God's Word and examine this truth.

Begin living your own adventure today. Risk something for Jesus. First listen, hear, then obey, just as you predetermined to do......

May Jesus fill you with boldness to begin. Look for the opportunities. They abound.

Maureen and I are 'Missionaries.' I have been a 'Missionary' in India, Mexico, Israel, Cyprus, various places in Asia, and America. Maureen in South Africa, Zimbabwe, Israel, Cyprus, and America. We are 'Missionaries' everywhere we go. Take note that we include our homeland as a place we act as Missionaries. Our neighborhood is always a mission field, no matter which country we happen to live in.

Included below is Maureen's favorite definition of 'A Missionary." (Taken from her second book, 'Assignment Love.')

A Missionary

A Missionary is anybody chosen by God, and not ourselves, to fulfil His commission.

Usually we do not fit into any recognized personality category. The man or woman must be born again, having had a real conversion experience.

Whatever else the Missionary may be doing, he is first and foremost, aware of his divine purpose for living, this being to touch and draw everybody by love to the Lord, who taught us to seek first the Kingdom of God and His righteousness and all else shall be added to us. This means that in thoughts, actions, words and deeds, we are to be ruled by godly principles.

Our mission is more important than our lives. That is the sign of a Missionary:

You will find these people all over the world: in lowly, in prominent, and frankly, in ridiculous places, serving the Lord where God has placed them. Such is the love of God, in Jesus Christ, to reach out and save the lost, that He chooses to use ordinary people like you and me, taking the foolish things of the world to confound the wise. What a magnificent Master Plan!

You too, are a Missionary. As Christians we are all Missionaries. Begin today, ask Father for opportunity to speak for Him to your neighbor, someone you meet on the street, in the Post Office, or at the market. Listen to them, hearing what is on their heart. Invite them to church. Offer to pray with them. Put aside your inhibitions, step out in boldness.

Once you do this, watch closely and begin to notice how God wants to touch others through you.

In Deuteronomy, 31:6, Moses says to Israel, *"be strong and courageous."* Then again in verse 7, he tells Joshua, *"be strong and courageous."* Then in verse 23, the Lord Himself tells Joshua, *"be strong and courageous."*

We see these exact words again in the very next book in the Bible, Joshua. Here the people of Israel exhorted Joshua to *"be strong and courageous."*

These words are for us today, we should do no less. Joshua was to cross the Jordan River and lead his people into the land that had been promised to them by their God, their Lord. The victory was assured, but strength and courage was needed, along with a boldness to take that first step into the Jordan. We require strength and courage, but our victory is assured. We simply must step out boldly into the enemies territory to claim what Father has said to take.

So, my friend, *'be strong and courageous,'* step into your Jordan, cross onto the adversaries turf, and help others take possession of their inheritance.

And remember......

"Our mission is more important than our lives. That is the sign of a Missionary."

Shouldn't we all be Missionaries?

In Closing

Maureen and Bill write to encourage Christians to greater heights in adventure for Kingdom sake. They desire to see Christians walk in love, integrity, single-mindedness, victory, and free of compromise. They also write that someone might come to realize the incredible hope found in Jesus Christ. Their lives are dedicated to these things.

Maureen and Bill are available to speak and travel anywhere, as the Lord leads.

Please feel free to write to:

Bill & Maureen Williamson
P.O. Box 1013
Payson, Arizona 85547
USA

Maureen's other books:

Audacity To Love
Assignment Love